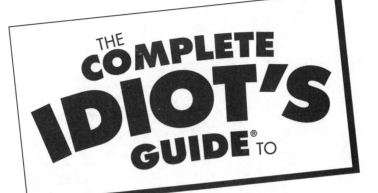

Backyard Adventures

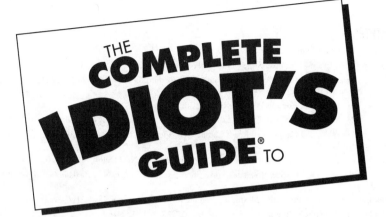

Backyard Adventures

by Nancy Worrell

ALPHA

A member of Penguin Group (USA) Inc.

ALPHA BOOKS

Published by the Penguin Group

Penguin Group (USA) Inc., 375 Hudson Street, New York, New York 10014, USA

Penguin Group (Canada), 90 Eglinton Avenue East, Suite 700, Toronto, Ontario M4P 2Y3, Canada (a division of Pearson Penguin Canada Inc.)

Penguin Books Ltd., 80 Strand, London WC2R 0RL, England

Penguin Ireland, 25 St. Stephen's Green, Dublin 2, Ireland (a division of Penguin Books Ltd.)

Penguin Group (Australia), 250 Camberwell Road, Camberwell, Victoria 3124, Australia (a division of Pearson Australia Group Pty. Ltd.)

Penguin Books India Pvt. Ltd., 11 Community Centre, Panchsheel Park, New Delhi—110 017, India

Penguin Group (NZ), 67 Apollo Drive, Rosedale, North Shore, Auckland 1311, New Zealand (a division of Pearson New Zealand Ltd.)

Penguin Books (South Africa) (Pty.) Ltd., 24 Sturdee Avenue, Rosebank, Johannesburg 2196, South Africa

Penguin Books Ltd., Registered Offices: 80 Strand, London WC2R 0RL, England

International Standard Book Number: 978-1-59257-757-6
Library of Congress Catalog Card Number: 2007941483

10   09   08   8   7   6   5   4   3   2   1

Interpretation of the printing code: The rightmost number of the first series of numbers is the year of the book's printing; the rightmost number of the second series of numbers is the number of the book's printing. For example, a printing code of 08–1 shows that the first printing occurred in 2008.

Printed in the United States of America

Note: This publication contains the opinions and ideas of its author. It is intended to provide helpful and informative material on the subject matter covered. It is sold with the understanding that the author and publisher are not engaged in rendering professional services in the book. If the reader requires personal assistance or advice, a competent professional should be consulted.

The author and publisher specifically disclaim any responsibility for any liability, loss, or risk, personal or otherwise, which is incurred as a consequence, directly or indirectly, of the use and application of any of the contents of this book.

Most Alpha books are available at special quantity discounts for bulk purchases for sales promotions, premiums, fund-raising, or educational use. Special books, or book excerpts, can also be created to fit specific needs.

For details, write: Special Markets, Alpha Books, 375 Hudson Street, New York, NY 10014.

Publisher: *Marie Butler-Knight*
Editorial Director: *Mike Sanders*
Senior Managing Editor: *Billy Fields*
Executive Editor: *Randy Ladenheim-Gil*
Development Editor: *Lynn Northrup*
Senior Production Editor: *Janette Lynn*

Copy Editor: *Lisanne V. Jensen*
Cover Designer: *Becky Harmon*
Book Designer: *Trina Wurst*
Layout: *Chad Dressler*
Proofreader: *Mary Hunt*

Bored children inspire mothers to be creative! This book is dedicated to my daughters and all our many backyard adventures.

Contents at a Glance

Contents

Introduction

Are you and your family always on the go but never seem to have much fun? Do you need some adventure in your lives? Why not plan a backyard adventure?

Too often, we look to someone—or somewhere—else for entertainment, education, and fun when all we need to do is open our eyes and explore our backyards. What's more, the experience doesn't have to be expensive or time-consuming. *The Complete Idiot's Guide to Backyard Adventures* is designed to help families explore and experience the adventure of natural wonders, athletic endeavors, cultural attractions, creative activities, and the fun and friendship of community that exists in our own backyards, neighborhoods, and towns.

You decide the actual adventure time—whether you want to spend a couple hours on an artistic activity or an entire summer producing a play. You design the activities around your family—their interests, age levels, skills, and abilities. Staying at home and experiencing an adventure in your backyard is so much easier than packing up your family members and heading off to someone else's version of adventureland. Not only do you bypass the hassle of getting there, but you also save time and money creating your own memories. A backyard adventure won't blow the budget. In fact, you may find you can afford to splurge on other activities.

This book offers fun tips on researching, planning, and executing great adventures. Customize adventures around family members, special interests, and available time and funds. Enjoy exploring one or all of these backyard adventures with your family!

What's in This Book

Whether you go on an insect safari, experience the past, make your own paper, venture on a neighborhood walkabout, or do one of the many other fun activities you'll find in this book, *The Complete Idiot's Guide to Backyard Adventures* is your guide to the pleasures that exist at home—in your backyard, neighborhood, and community.

I also include two appendixes: Appendix A lists suggested books and websites related to the activities in each chapter, and Appendix B lists some wonderful, wacky holidays you and your family may wish to celebrate.

Extras

Sprinkled throughout this book are three types of sidebars that offer interesting facts, helpful tips, and cautions. Here's what to look for:

Did You Know?

These boxes contain tidbits of trivia and fun facts associated with the related adventure.

Way to Go!

These hints and tips help you make the most of your adventure.

Easy Does It

These boxes offer cautions to make sure you have a fun and safe adventure.

Acknowledgments

Thanks to everyone who has helped make this book possible. To my editors, what a great job you did of making me look good! Thank you.

Trademarks

All terms mentioned in this book that are known to be or are suspected of being trademarks or service marks have been appropriately capitalized. Alpha Books and Penguin Group (USA) Inc. cannot attest to the accuracy of this information. Use of a term in this book should not be regarded as affecting the validity of any trademark or service mark.

1

The Adventure Begins

In This Chapter

- ◆ Fun and family time in your own backyard
- ◆ It's all in the planning
- ◆ What makes a great adventure?
- ◆ Do some research

Summer holidays and vacation time is often spent seeking adventure in someone else's backyard. But actual adventure time is often cut short by two or more days spent traveling to the destination of choice. Wouldn't it be wonderful to grab a couple "extra" days to play? Save time and bypass the hassle of getting there—not to mention the expense of looking for adventure beyond the boundaries of your backyard. A backyard adventure won't blow the budget. In fact, you may find you can afford to enjoy several adventures because you have more time and fewer expenses. You can make every day an adventure at home. This book offers tips on researching, planning, and executing great adventures in your own community. You can customize adventures around family members, special interests, available time, and funds. So … let the adventures begin!

Home Is Where the Fun Is

Backyard adventures involve learning, experiencing new things, and having fun at home with family. In the hustle and bustle of today's world, we are constantly running to work, to school, to practice, to the gym, to lessons, and so on. There's always something to do, and we just don't take time to smell the roses. The roses I'm talking about are the quiet, personal times you could be spending at home with family doing things together. I'm also talking about the roses that are overgrown in your backyard because you just haven't had any time to spend there. Take a few minutes to see whether you can remember the last time your entire family sat down to dinner together or played together. (Vacation time and holidays don't count.) We're talking about the everyday experiences that could very well be wonderful adventures along your life's journey.

Did You Know?

♦ The average U.S. household spends 5.1 percent of its income on entertainment.

♦ The average cost per night for a hotel room is $98.

♦ On average, a vacation for a family of four costs $261 per day for food and lodging.

♦ Sports camps can cost upward of $1,000 for one week.

Next time you're in a panic to find something to entertain the kids—or when grandparents come to visit or if you're just planning something special to do on the weekend—stop and take a look in your backyard and your community. The backyard is perfect for a botany adventure, planting a garden, or camping out. Think about your family's various interests. From bugs to art to performing, all things kids enjoy can also be shared with family members—making for a great entertaining day, weekend, or entire week. Do you really need to look any farther for an adventure?

Plan for Success

Any adventure requires some planning, teamwork, and cooperative effort to be a success. It means that as a family, you learn to communicate, work together, and ultimately share a fun backyard adventure. Pick one or two activities that really fit your family. You may want to revise or adapt it so that it works better for your family members in particular. And remember, these can be little or big adventures. An adventure can be as simple as learning about a different culture (see Chapter 4) or as elaborate as planning and executing a block party with the neighbors (see Chapter 6). The idea is to look at some everyday things and see how they can actually become a shared adventure.

For those of us who live in the country or suburbia, we truly can plan a backyard adventure. City dwellers, however, don't fret; many of these backyard adventures can be adapted to a nearby park, greenway, or vacant lot. Take a close look at your surroundings and consider the many backyard

Easy Does It

Don't try to do everything in one adventure. Spread out your activities over a period of time. That way, you can concentrate on making one adventure at a time a success.

adventures that are available—from an insect safari (see Chapter 2) to stargazing (see Chapter 2). An old-fashioned, all-day picnic with games (see Chapter 2) qualifies as a mini adventure. Building a fort or camping out (see Chapter 2) over the weekend is a great group activity that breaks the monotony. And don't forget to include your neighbors in the fun; ask them to attend an ice cream social or participate in a pet parade (see Chapter 6).

Family Meeting

Part of the fun of any adventure is in the anticipation. You will want to include the entire family in the planning process, being sure to provide something of interest for each member to explore, enjoy, and remember. You can begin by asking everyone to think of things they would like to do, experience, or learn. Keep a running list. Small children are sure to have small, easy requests (such as riding a pony or building a fort). Older children will have bigger, more elaborate ideas for an adventure—such as learning or improving on a sport, riding a skateboard, or going on a camping trip. Schedule a planning meeting asking everyone to bring their ideas to discuss.

Set a time to meet and discuss everyone's ideas. Use your running list to get started, then ask each family member to share additional suggestions for an adventure. Have a brainstorming session and list anything and everything that pops into your heads. Nothing is off limits at this point. This is a great time to have fun imagining the possibilities. It's also a good way for families to get to know more about each other's dreams!

Way to Go!

Remember that adventures mean different things to different people and age groups. While a day with a choice of 31 flavors of ice cream and playing in the sprinkler sounds like heaven to a young child, teenagers may visualize a day of skipping school, lying around in pajamas, watching videos, playing games, and eating pizza.

Organize the lists into Activities, Exploring, Sharing, Learning, Holidays or Parties, and Individual. Add any other topics that seem appropriate; for example:

◆ Activities: Plant a garden (see Chapter 5) or fly a kite (see Chapter 2).

◆ Exploring: Go on an insect safari (see Chapter 2) or take a walkabout (see Chapter 7).

◆ Sharing: Lend a hand (see Chapter 4) or have dinner on the ground (see Chapter 6).

◆ Learning: Make paper or celebrate your town's local history (see Chapter 7).

◆ Holidays or parties: Have a block party (see Chapter 6).

◆ Individual: Hold training camp (see Chapter 3) or explore artistic activities (see Chapter 5).

Once you have the list, go through it and ask everyone to pick the top five adventures they want to share as a family. They may also want to pick the top five adventures they personally are interested in doing.

Getting It Down on Paper

Now that you've picked some adventures, you will need a way of organizing the information. Before the planning session, make idea forms. Have space for the title of your adventure. Under the title, set up columns for General Information, Resources, Equipment/Supplies, Activities, Food, Memories, and Miscellaneous.

For example, if your family chooses camping out under General Information, you would list logistics such as where, when, and who is participating. Under Resources, list the names of anyone you know who can provide information about tents and how to set one up (assuming that camp-

Easy Does It

Don't insist that everyone participate in the planning process. It just may not be their thing. Do make sure at some point they get to do something they want.

ing out is a totally new adventure for your family). Equipment/Supplies would include a tent, sleeping bags, flashlights, and anything else you'll need for your camping adventure. You will probably want to do more than just camp out, though. Incorporate other adventures—such as stargazing or an insect safari. List these adventures under Activities along with telling ghost stories or singing camp songs. Food is obvious; of course, you want food like hot dogs and marshmallows for s'mores. In your Memories column, list ways to record the fun. It may be through taking digital photographs, making a video of putting up the tent, or recording yourselves as you sing camp songs. In the Miscellaneous column, jot down any other details about the adventure—this is a good place to start a shopping list.

If you list any other activities you want to incorporate into this backyard adventure, then create another sheet with the same kind of lists—filling in the columns that apply to that activity. Now you've planned for a successful adventure!

Elements of a Great Adventure

An adventure is defined as an unusual or exciting experience. Unusual and exciting are the operable words and are only relative to what you have done or experienced. For young children, every day is a new adventure—even if it means having to pick themselves up off the side-walk a dozen times that day. As adults, we tend to think of every day as a new challenge or problem—not seeing the excitement and totally missing the element of adventure in the daily chores of life. Let's open our eyes to the wonderful possibility of adventures in our own back-yards.

Initially, you should set aside a specific time for your big adventure so that you can devote all your time, energy, and concentration to it. Immerse yourself, so to speak. Start with alerting the neighbors, your boss and coworkers, and friends and relatives that you are not available during that time. This means no phone calls, no errands, and no visits unless they're invited to participate. You'll want to suspend regular chores and bedtimes and be sure to relax the rules. Don't bring work home from the office or plan to clean out the attic or garage—either one spoils the essence of adventure!

How long should your adventure be? One of the great things about a backyard adventure is that it fits your family's schedule. You will decide how much time you have for an adventure. Several mini adventures may be just the ticket for your family, especially if your children attend year-round school. You may want to set aside a week or several long weekends. Keep in mind that staying at home or close to home frees up additional time for the actual adventure.

Part of what makes a great adventure is being able to remember it and share your experiences with others. Take lots of photos and use your scanner and computer to create your own picture postcards. Take your photos to your local copy shop and have them enlarged into posters or made into calendars. Let the little ones draw a picture that represents their adventure, and share their artwork with grandparents. If you have a video camera, take lots of footage. Enjoy your summer water adven-ture next winter when the wind is howling outside.

Way to Go!

Your backyard adventures don't have to end. Plan future activities around editing videos and making photo postcards or handmade greeting cards. Creative projects make wonderful gifts or can be used as original artistic creations to decorate your room, home, or office.

Make your backyard adventure memorable by keeping a journal and collecting memorabilia for a scrapbook. Jot down notes of special feelings, little things that happened, and what the weather was like. Be as descriptive as possible to help you relive the moment. Save your idea forms, resource material, and pressed leaves or flowers to include in your scrapbook. Write descriptive letters to yourself about your adventure. Add drawings to narratives and notes next to photos and other memorabilia. Months and years later, you will be able to relive those special moments through your photos, videos, journals, and scrapbooks.

Do Your Homework

As a family, you selected several ideas from the brainstorming session. Now it's time to do the research. While there is lots of information on the Internet, don't forget to browse the stacks of books at the library or your local bookstore. Look for books and magazines that focus of your adventure. (See Appendix A for some suggested books and websites to get you started.) There is a plethora of do-it-yourself books and television shows available. You can learn to bake bread, make paper or soap, knit, sew, paint, build a tree house or pond, and create kites or paper airplanes. The local bookstore may have a guest how-to author demonstrating a technique from his or her latest book. Specialty shops and grocery stores occasionally offer cooking classes. Contact your hobby, craft, fabric, needlework, gardening, or hardware store for a list of classes.

Is there a local art guild? In some areas, artists will open their studios once a year for tours. There's no better way to see an artist at work than in his or her own studio. Is there a local drama group? Contact them to find out about presentations. Invite a local expert to lunch or dinner and ask him or her to share expertise in that particular area. Perhaps your child's favorite science teacher can help you identify the insects living in your yard. You could invite a gardener or farmer to help you plan a great vegetable, herb, or flower garden. You may know a geologist who can help you classify your collection of rocks. Ask an amateur astronomer to point out constellations and planets.

Contact local nonprofit and government agencies for information. The county cooperative extension agency is a good source of information on gardening and plants. The chamber of commerce or tourism bureau can offer lots of information about historical sites, special events such as farm or studio tours, as well as general information about your town. While you are there, ask about maps for walking and bike trails and schedules of upcoming concerts, craft fairs, and festivals. Look for information on ethnic festivals and cultural events. Pick up event calendars and see what's available in your area.

Museums are another good source of information. Often, smaller museums don't have as many visitors and can spend more time with you talking about the exhibits. In larger cities or metropolitan areas, you can contact local museums for a list of scheduled events, showings, openings, classes, or lectures. Many museums have special events to promote a new exhibit. A special guest is often asked to teach a class, give a slide presentation, or lecture to promote the exhibit. Many of these events focus on children's interests and many of these events are free.

Check with the local parks and recreation department for a schedule of classes, sports teams, and sporting events. Your local parks and recreation department may offer classes in drama, dance, or Chinese calligraphy. Some parks and recreation departments will offer sports camps. If there is a university or junior college in your area, check their community calendars for special events and classes. Do you have a local stable where you can learn to ride? Does the nearby ski resort offer special day passes and/or classes for the community?

Way to Go!

What kinds of businesses are in your area? Do you have a bike manufacturer, a candy factory, a dairy farm, an incredible bakery, or a local newspaper? Contact that business to see whether it offers tours. What better way to learn about something than experiencing it firsthand?

If you are interested in discovering more about your town, find out whether there is an historical event that took place. Check with the local library, historical or preservation society, or the city paper. Is your house located on the old campgrounds of a Native American tribe? Did famous explorers Lewis and Clark follow a trail through your neighborhood? What is the story behind the deserted Victorian house on the hill? Was there a civil war battle fought in your county? Were gold or silver found in the streams or hills nearby? Have you ever taken the time to read the historical markers you pass each day?

There is plenty of information available for just about any adventure you choose. Do a little research, and make your backyard adventure a wonderful experience.

It's time for adventure. Explore the possibilities that are offered in your very own backyard. Make some plans, do the research, and let the adventure begin!

Chapter 2

Your Corner of the World

In This Chapter

- Kids love bugs!
- Flower or weed?
- A backyard hideaway
- A star-studded event
- A gem of an adventure
- Flyaway fun with kites
- Picnic fun

Step outside into your backyard and explore your little corner of the world. Using a bit of imagination and ingenuity, you can plan an insect safari, explore the universe, and delve into the mysteries of the heavens—all in your backyard.

Do you long to experience nightlife or explore a deserted island? With a sprinkle of stardust and make-believe, you can fulfill those desires in your own backyard by camping under the stars or hunting for rocks.

These are just a few suggestions to get you started seeing your backyard as a place of discovery, adventure, and fun. You can also share the experience with your family and friends.

See Appendix A for suggested books and websites relating to the activities in this chapter.

Insect Safari

Kids love bugs! Plan an insect safari. As portrayed in recent Hollywood movies, bugs have very interesting lives. Plan an expedition to look for insects in the backyard or garden, at the park, or during a hike in the woods. Go to the library or bookstore and pick up some books to identify various insects. In the planning stage, you may want to enlist the help of your local science teacher or cooperative extension agent in locating information on the types of insects that may be found in your area.

Depending on your locale and the season, some times may be better than others to find a large variety of insects. During summer months, early morning and late afternoon into evening will most likely yield the largest variety of bugs. Examine tree branches, the underside of plant leaves, under rocks, and dig into the dirt to find out which insects exist in your backyard.

What You'll Need

- Books on insects
- White cardstock and clean jars (baby food jars are excellent)
- A magnifying glass
- A notebook and pencil; crayons or colored markers
- A trowel (optional)
- Gloves (optional)
- A digital camera (optional)

Did You Know?

♦ There are more than one million described species of insects.

♦ Insects have lived for some 200 million years.

♦ Insects are related to crabs and lobsters.

♦ Most insects are beneficial because they eat other insects, pollinate crops, are food for other animals, make products like honey and silk, or have medical uses.

♦ Insects have skeletons on the outside of their bodies (called exoskeletons).

♦ A cockroach can live for nine days without a head.

♦ The cochineal insect is a source of natural red dye.

♦ An adult head louse becomes the color of the person's hair in which it lives.

♦ An ant can pull 50 times its own weight.

♦ Grasshoppers can jump 40 times their length.

♦ A bee may fly up to 60 miles in one day to find food.

You can carry your magnifying glass, books, notebook, and pencil along with you and identify bugs on the spot. Being careful not to injure the insect, scoop it up onto the white cardstock and carefully examine it in a shady area using the magnifying glass. Gently return the bug to its habitat once you've identified it. If you find a dead bug you can carefully put it in a jar to protect its fragile body parts and take it home for later examination. Page through your books, brochures, or other information you may have about the bugs in your area and try to identify each one. Keep a list of the bugs you identify in your notebook, listing the kind of bug, where it was found, the date and time, and any other information you may consider significant. It will depend on the age and interest of the child as far as how in depth this examination should be.

Easy Does It

Don't pick up any living bugs using your fingers. You don't want to get pinched by a beetle or stung by a wasp. Also, insects are fragile—and you may damage a wing or break a leg if you pick one up.

Small children love to draw. Let them carry crayons, colored pencils, or markers along for drawing the various bugs in their notebooks. Ask them to draw what the bug eats. Have them play a game of imagining what they might see if they were bug-size.

Older children will want to examine their habitat and learn about eating habits, life cycle, and expectancy of the various insects. Have a conversation about which bugs are beneficial or harmful and why. Stake out a one-foot square of your backyard or garden area—a cool, damp, shady area is best—and have them record the life that exists within that square foot over a period of time, whether it's for the day or for the year. Are the same insects in that square in the evening as in the morning? Are there more or fewer at different times of the day? Do they live on the plants, under a rock, or in the ground? What is their enemy? Have them imagine a day in their little corner of the world and write a short story about the insect's life. It can be serious and analytical, talking about how these insects interact to survive. Or let their imaginations run wild with a flight of fanciful flies.

If you have a digital camera, you can record your wonderful finds and use them for reference and research (maybe for that science project you know you have to do next fall). Consider the following questions. What are the insects' feeding habits, habitats, and life cycle? Which caterpillars will turn into butterflies, and which ones will become moths? Which insects are beneficial, and how do they make your garden grow? Create a scrapbook of photos. Under the photo of each insect, list its common name and scientific name, what it eats, and how long it lives. If you have photos of larvae and butterflies, show both on the same page so next time you will know which larva turns into which butterfly. Children who show a real interest in this activity may want to return monthly or seasonally to see whether anything has changed.

Or you can just have fun with the photos, uploading them to your computer and creating works of art—from a colorful collection of greeting cards and fun stickers to a poster worthy of framing.

An insect safari can be a fascinating and educational backyard adventure.

Backyard Botany

Take a long look at your backyard. How many plants are there? (When I say plants, I mean everything with roots, such as trees, flowers, bushes, grasses, weeds, and vines.) How many of these plants can you identify? Which ones are weeds or native plants? What plants were planted in your yard by your family or the previous tenant? Spend a beautiful summer afternoon exploring the backyard, discovering all the lovely unusual plants living there. Look beyond the green to the leaves and flowers.

What You'll Need

- ◆ Books on flowers and plants
- ◆ A sketchbook and pencil; colored pencils or markers
- ◆ Envelopes, a scrapbook, or a flower press
- ◆ Scissors or shears
- ◆ A magnifying glass
- ◆ A digital camera (optional)

Before you begin your botany adventure, make a map of your yard or the area that you plan to explore. Draw in the trees, rocks, edge of the house, and sidewalk—noting flower beds and bushes. Once you have a map of the area, you can begin to identify the flora within. Divide the area map into sections, and number each section. You can then use those section numbers in your notes to identify where you found the plants.

Now the fun begins. Use a pair of scissors or shears to clip off leaves and flowers, putting them in envelopes noting the location using your section number. You can examine the plants in detail and make notes on your envelope. Later, you will want to search your reference books to identify each cutting.

Did You Know?

♦ Many so-called weeds are just plants that we don't have an immediate use for or that have become invasive.

♦ Dandelions can be served as exotic greens or made into wine.

♦ Purple coneflower, also known as Echinacea, is often used to treat colds and the flu.

♦ Red and white clover add nitrogen to the soil.

♦ Milkweed attracts monarch butterflies.

♦ Morning glories can take over a field or embellish a gardener's fence or trellis.

♦ Whether you consider Queen Anne's lace a wild-flower or a weed, it makes a lovely addition to a perennial garden.

You can also clip the leaves and flowers and put them into a scrapbook or between papers for your flower press. On the scrapbook page or the flower press paper, note the yard section number where you found the plant, the date, and time of day. You may also want to note the color of the flowers because the color may change as they dry. Later in the season, return to see whether there are new flowers or seed heads or whether the leaves have changed color.

Sketching plants can be fun for young and old alike. Take a sketch-book, and colored pencils or markers with you on your exploration of the backyard. The little ones will delight in drawing flowers with all their bright colors, adding a few green leaves and a beautiful blue-sky background. Older kids can use a drawing pencil and create wonderful black-and-white pencil drawings of the delicate flower petals, identify-ing the different parts of the flower and plant.

Collect seeds for planting. For little ones, let them plant a bean or sunflower in a small paper cup. Instead of dirt, put a damp cotton ball in the bottom of the cup and keep it moist. Sit it on a low windowsill where they can check on the growth everyday. How very exciting to observe the very beginning of the seed cracking open to that first hint of roots pushing out of the shell—growing into a tiny green plant!

Older children may enjoy having a flower bed or garden of their own in the yard. A couple square feet in a sunny place is more than enough space for a first observation garden. Start with letting them collect seeds and cuttings from plants in and around your backyard. They can plant them in their space, noting which grow from seeds and which can be rooted and grown from plant cuttings.

Using reference books to identify wildflowers, perennials, weeds, shrubs, and trees, you can start a catalog of the plant life in your backyard—noting where these plants are located in the various sections on your backyard map.

Easy Does It

Leaves of three, let them be! Be careful not to touch poison ivy in your quest to identify plants.

Learn which plants are native to your backyard and will be easiest to grow based on climate. Identify what type of fruit or berry is produced. Find out which plants will attract birds or butterflies or repel mosquitoes. Some plants thrive when planted next to each other (called companion planting). Believe it or not, carrots love to grow next to tomatoes.

After spending time in your backyard identifying plants, go on a hike or take a walk through a park to see whether you can find plants similar to the ones in your backyard. Make it a game, competing to see who can identify the most plants during your walk.

Collect, press, and dry flowers, leaves, seeds, and stems for other projects. Newsprint is great for drying and pressing flower petals. The pressed flowers are wonderful for making cards or framing in tiny frames. Identify various herbs and dry them for later use in a wonderful winter soup. Bits and pieces of dried flowers and leaves can be used in other projects such as papermaking (see Chapter 5).

Consider using a digital camera to take snapshots of the plant as well as of the leaves and flowers. You can use these photographs to identify your backyard plants. You may also want to choose the most interesting ones, enlarge them, and frame them for a special place in your house and as a wonderful reminder of your backyard botany adventure.

You will be surprised at how many plants you can identify!

Backyard Hideaway

Camping is a great backyard adventure. If you have small children or you are first-time campers, don't set yourself up for unforgettable surprises far from home. Do a trial-run camping trip in your backyard. Then, if it rains or the night noises are just too much, you can always retreat to the house and try another time. This is also a great time to figure out how the tent is set up or how hard the ground really is. Novice campers can enjoy the experience close to home, and for the seasoned camper it can be an opportunity to enjoy the outdoors when you really don't have the time or are unable to hike into the high country. Camping out changes your daily routine and gets you out of the house and away from the phone and the noise of your busy lives—but not too far from hot, running water and the convenience of a bathroom.

What You'll Need

- Tent or a tarp with rope and stakes
- Sleeping bags
- A grill or camp stove
- A child's swimming pool (optional)
- Hot dogs, buns, and condiments
- Skewers
- Graham crackers, large marshmallows, and chocolate bars for s'mores

Survey your backyard for a suitable campsite. You may have a wonderful secluded area under some trees, or you may decide to go for the most distant corner of the backyard. Choose a place that's level, and stake it out. If you have a tent, put it up. If not—and you have to improvise with a rope tied between two trees—you will have to opt for the two trees that fit the bill. After tying a rope between the two trees, drape a tarp or piece of canvas over the rope and secure it at each corner with stakes. Need a body of water nearby? Fill a child's swimming pool and declare it "the lake." You might want to add a rubber duck, a small sailboat, or little plastic fish.

Did You Know?

♦ Camping was an original way of life. Nomadic tribes moved from place to place, taking their homes (tents) with them.

♦ Early tents were made out of animal skins, felt, and canvas.

♦ There is evidence of tents being used 40,000 years ago.

♦ According to the Travel Industry Association, camping is the number one outdoor vacation activity in America.

♦ The first recorded recipe for s'mores is found in *Scouting for Girls* (1927 edition).

Now that your site is set up with a tent, a place to sleep, and of course "the lake," it is time to think about food. Set up a grill or camp stove for cooking. (Do not build a campfire in your backyard without first checking with your local fire department.) And what better to have during a campout than hot dogs and toasted marshmallows and/or s'mores?

Organize camp crafts and games, tell fireside stories, or have a sing-along. Hikes around the yard or in the neighborhood are in order. You may even want to go on an insect safari (as described earlier in this chapter). And if spending the night in the tent isn't a reality just yet, definitely plan to spend an evening under the stars.

If it's more than camping out you want, make your own hideaway, teepee, tent, or tree house. Be creative. Pile tree branches and twigs together to form a green igloo. A large appliance box with cutout windows and a door makes a great temporary fort (especially good for young children). Young children love indoor tents. Push kitchen, dining room, or outdoor chairs together to form a square or circle and drape a big blanket over the chairs for a fun hiding spot.

Way to Go!

To make a s'more, toast a large marshmallow over hot coals until it's crispy and gooey. Lay it on one half of a graham cracker, cover with half of a chocolate bar, and place the other half of the graham cracker on top—pressing together slightly to melt the chocolate.

If you have the time, you may want to spend several weekends and build a more permanent getaway. Recycle leftover building materials to build that dream hideaway in the sky: a tree house. With patience, a green thumb, and the experience of a botany adventure, you may decide to "grow" a teepee. Prop up PVC pipe or bamboo poles to form a teepee shape. For a summer teepee, plant a variety of climbing plants such as beans, morning glories, or sweet-scented moonflowers around the base of the teepee shape. Train the vines up the poles, and keep the inside trimmed. Of course, you could plant longer-lasting woody vines such as honeysuckle or grapes and have a teepee that gets better with age. Determine what fits your needs, time, age group, and your budget—and be creative with building your special hideaway!

Stargazing

When was the last time you noticed the full moon or looked for constellations in the night sky? If you live in a large city, it may be difficult to see the stars because of all the surrounding lights. If you live in the country, maybe you have just been too busy to notice them. What a glorious phenomenon you have been missing!

What You'll Need

- Book and maps of the sky

- Lounge chair(s) and/or blankets

- A compass

- Binoculars or a telescope

- Insect repellent (for summer months)

Before you start, find a map that shows the night sky with its constellations for your locale and the current season. Identify the constellations you want to find, and make a list for your stargazing night.

A fun activity for young and old alike—and a good way to become more familiar with the constellations—is to make pin-punched models of the constellations. Pick out the constellations from a book. Using white chalk, lightly sketch the constellation on a piece of black construction paper, noting where each star is located. Using a sewing needle or hat pin, punch a tiny hole for each star. Turn off all the lights except for a lamp with a large white shade that is easily accessible. Hold or clip the black paper to the shade, and turn on the light to see your pinpoint constellation.

Now, let's look at the real thing. Locate a good clearing away from trees and bright lights, and set up your outdoor chairs or spread a blanket on the ground. For young children, start early enough in the evening so that they can look for that "first star I see tonight." They will watch in awe as the sky fills with more and more stars and that big yellow moon. Using a compass, find true north. Situate the map with designated north pointing to the north you have identified. On a dark, clear, moonless night, 1,000 or more stars are visible. Initially, using only your eyes and your map of the night sky, see how many constellations you can identify. As you locate each one, check it off the list you made earlier. Learn where the North Star (Polaris) is so that you will never get lost. See whether you can identify any planets, satellites, or even the space station. Look for the Milky Way. Use a telescope or binoculars to look for the rings of Saturn or the valleys on the moon.

Watch the news or check out astronomy websites to find out when the next meteor shower or eclipse of the moon will be visible in your area. Plan a special meteor shower or eclipse party. Find where the best viewing area is for the special event. Make sure city lights or trees will not obscure your view. Set up your chairs; bring the blankets, food, and drink; and invite family, friends, and neighbors to join you for this star-studded event.

Did You Know?

- The night sky is divided into 88 constellations.

- Constellations and planet positions vary from season to season.

- The Milky Way, our galaxy, is most impressive in the summer.

- Most constellation objects and names come from Greek and Roman myths.

- Locate the Big Dipper in the northern sky, and use those stars to locate one or two important constellations for each season.

- In the spring, look for Gemini (the twins) and Leo (the Lion).

- Summer constellations to look for are Scorpius (the scorpion) and Sagittarius (the archer).

- Pegasus, the winged horse, is visible during autumn months.

- The clear winter sky showcases Orion (the hunter) and Taurus (the bull).

- Planets visible from Earth without a telescope are Venus, Mars, Jupiter, and Saturn.

- Meteor showers occur annually. Check with your local planetarium for dates when they are visible from your backyard.

Beyond the stargazing night, you may want take a trip to a planetarium to learn more about our night sky. Older children can research how early explorers navigated by the stars and can plot a map of their neighborhood. There may be a budding astronaut in the family after a few fun-filled nights of stargazing.

Rock Hounds

There is more to rocks then meets the eye. Take time to collect and learn about the different kinds of rocks. Rocks tell a story. You may live on the remains of an ancient sea, lake, or forest. The rocks that are common in your area will tell the tale. Rocks may not be the only find, too. It takes a little research and time, but you will soon learn to identify rocks that are really petrified wood, bits of fossilized bone or shell, hardened lava, or minerals.

A good place to start is checking out books about rocks and learning about the various kinds of rocks (igneous, sedimentary, fossils, and metamorphic). A trip to a local museum may provide clues to the topography and origins of your corner of the world. Craft fairs may be another good source of information, because at least one exhibitor often comes with polished and unpolished rocks. Not only can you see and learn about various rocks, but you can also see how they look in the raw and then after they are polished. If the vendor lives nearby, arrange a visit to learn more about identifying, collecting, and polishing rocks.

What You'll Need

- A small trowel

- A pouch for carrying your finds

- Books for identifying your rocks

- Rock tumbler (optional)

You can plan a rock hunting excursion, or you can just take time during your daily walk to look down and see what is underfoot. Pick up a few rocks that catch your eye to take home and identify. A great time for finding new and different rocks is after a big rain. Often, the rain will wash away the mud and dirt—and the rocks hiding beneath will be exposed. If someone has been digging, whether for planting or building, sift through the dirt to see what may have been unearthed when the dirt was turned over. Even the gravel dumped on driveways can produce some unusual gems. Watch for unusual rocks when you are walking to school or the park, hiking a trail, or just digging in the garden. All of these places are excellent for finding rocks.

Easy Does It

Be careful turning over large rocks during your hunt. You could squish a finger or toe, and you have no idea what creepy-crawly animal may be beneath that rock.

To begin with, you and your young children may want to collect only rocks that sparkle or are all pink. Put the collection in a clear glass jar so you all can admire the finds.

Older children will be more interested in picking up rocks that look interesting and then identifying them. Eventually, they may want to create a special box for holding the rocks—each identified with its name and the location where it was found. You could also add the date when the rock was found (which gives something to reminisce about: "When I found ...").

Did You Know?

♦ Igneous rocks come from magma—molten mixtures of minerals such as volcanic rocks. These rocks include micas, feldspar, quartz, and granite (a combination of quartz, feldspar, and mica). Other igneous rocks are glassy black obsidian and lightweight pumice.

♦ Sedimentary rocks are a result of materials being moved from one place to another by running water, wind, waves, currents, ice, and gravity. These rocks are made up of grains or particles of sand, mud, and fossils. Common examples of sedimentary rocks are sandstone, limestone, shale, and conglomerate.

♦ Fossils are the remains or impressions of former plant or animal life found naturally buried in rocks. Examples of fossils are impressions of ferns or shells in rocks, petrified wood, and decomposed materials resulting in deposits of coal.

♦ Metamorphic rocks are rocks that have changed—usually into a new crystalline structure. Metamorphism is the result of heat, pressure, or permeation by other substances. Metamorphic rocks include slate, marble, and quartzite.

Of course, there is more to just finding, identifying, and collecting rocks in a box. You may have a budding gemologist in the family who would enjoy having a rock tumbler for polishing rocks—changing them from raw earthen finds into beautiful, shiny gems suitable for making into jewelry or just admiring.

Rocks are everywhere, but when has your family taken the time to look down and see the beauties that they are? Have a gem-dandy adventure hunting rocks.

Go Fly a Kite

Has anyone ever told you to "Go fly a kite"? So, why not have a great adventure doing just that? Kites today come in a multitude of sizes, shapes, and colors. Some basic kite shapes are the diamond, box, winged box, and bat. The more complex designs include the UFO circoflex (a circle) and the tetrahedral (four-sided) kites. There are Japanese, Chinese, decorative, and competition kites. Kites are made from paper, plastic, and cloth (including silk). Kites may be a single color or covered in intricate designs from dragons to butterflies to a kid's favorite superhero.

Building and flying kites is an adventure with which your entire family can get involved. You can start with the simple diamond-shaped kites that you build out of paper and balsa wood and move onto the more elaborate box kites. There are numerous books and websites that have history and information about various kites as well as instructions for building your very own kite (see Appendix A). You can also find kite kits. Once your family members get involved with kites, they may want to attend kite festivals and join or start a kite club.

What You'll Need

- A ready-made kite or assorted materials for building and decorating a kite

- String

Begin by learning about different types of kites, the material used to make them, and the different parts of a kite. You may want to buy a simple kite and learn how to fly one before you attempt to build your own. For small, inexpensive kites you build yourself, you can use materials such as plastic or paper shopping bags, newspaper, and craft or wrapping paper. For the spine and crossbar, you can use bamboo or wood skewers. For larger kites, try using balsa wood or small wooden dowels. Fabric scraps or plastic bag scraps can be used for the tail for stabilization. Tie the ball of string to the kite, and you're ready to fly!

Did You Know?

- The Chinese began building and flying kites more than 2,000 years ago.

- In ancient China, kites were used to ward off evil spirits and scare away enemies.

- Originally, kites were used in various religious and cultural ceremonies—but later, kites were used for scientific experiments (Benjamin Franklin's is the most well known) and for fun.

- Letters and newspapers were delivered using kites during the American Civil War.

- Kites can be used to scare away birds.

- The fastest recorded speed of a kite is more than 120 mph.

- More than 50 million kites are sold each year in the United States.

- More adults in the world fly kites than children.

If you decide to make your own kites, you will want to consider the age of the children participating. For small children, cut out the diamond shape and put all the pieces together in a kit form. The little ones will have great fun decorating their own kites but will probably need help with assembly. That's where the older children can get involved. Once they figure out how to attach and assemble a kite and tie the strings, they can help the little ones build their own. So before the assembly, provide markers for drawing designs on the plastic. You can use markers, crayons, or paint for paper kites. A cold, blustery day in late winter or early spring is a great time to make kites. You can make several kites while anticipating the warm, breezy days of spring when you can fly them.

Of course, making a kite is only half the fun. The entire point of the adventure is to have a kite that flies. For fun, note the length of the string ball for each kite. If you have 100 feet and are holding the very end of the string, you know your kite is flying 100 feet away. You might want to keep a tally sheet to see whose kite goes the farthest.

You can also compete to see who can get their kite up and flying the quickest. Try making lots of little kites and stringing them together. Who has the most kites flying at one time?

Easy Does It

Play it safe. Never fly kites near trees, power lines, or airports!

For older children, learning the aerodynamics of why kites fly will be both helpful in making and flying them—and inadvertently teaching them some scientific principles of flying. In order for a kite to fly, it must be at the correct angle for the wind to force the kite up. Therefore, it's important that the string is attached to the kite at the right point. If the string is too high, the kite will not have enough lift to fly. If the string is attached too low, there will be drag on the kite and it will not fly. Of course, you do have to have some wind for the lift to happen. If there's no wind, then you will have to create your own. Run, run, run!

March is always thought of as kite-flying month, but that isn't necessarily true. If you live near the beach, you almost always have a suitable breeze for flying a kite. That is also true if you live out west, where there is often a breeze blowing across the prairie. So, get together with family and friends and "go fly a kite."

Blanket and a Basket

Picnics never go out of style. Whether it's a grand picnic with a white tablecloth and candelabra (as was the tradition of the moveable outdoor feasts of times gone by) or just pizza and soft drinks at the park, there is something glorious and fun about eating outside. A picnic can be an all-day adventure with lots of food, family, fun, and games. A picnic can also be incorporated with other adventures, such as stargazing and bike riding. All ages—from the tiniest tots to the grownups—always seem to enjoy the fun of a picnic.

What You'll Need

♦ Quilt or blanket, or waterproof tarp if the ground is damp

♦ Picnic basket or lunchbox packed with goodies, utensils, and napkins

♦ Bug spray

♦ Sunscreen

Make the picnic a family event and fill an old-fashioned basket with fried chicken, potato salad, and baked beans to bring back the nostalgia of picnics during your grandmother's era. To add to the fun, you can set up a croquet set, badminton net, or hold 3-legged races. Entertain the little ones with old-fashioned games like hide-and-seek. Indulge in watermelon and have a seed-spitting contest. After all the fun and games, retire to a blanket under a shady tree for iced tea or frosty lemonade, a good book, and maybe even a nap. Pack read-aloud books and/or crayons and coloring books for some quiet entertainment for the little ones.

Or keep it simple with milk and cookies on an old quilt under a shade tree on a hot summer afternoon. A lazy summer afternoon interlude can offer a respite from the dog days of summer and the busy technological lives we all lead.

Easy Does It

Adhere to safety precautions! Keep hot food hot and cold food cold. Don't let food requiring refrigeration (such as deviled eggs, milk, and potato salad) sit out for longer than two hours.

For an elegant picnic with a 1950s theme, fix little tea sandwiches filled with cucumber slices and cream cheese and serve lemonade in frosty-cold glasses on a floral tablecloth spread across the picnic table. This would make for a fun picnic for pre-teen girls. They may want to bring or make hats and choose who comes with the most creative, biggest, or most outlandish hat.

A change in the lunch routine could be a simple picnic for the little ones, offering tiny peanut butter and jelly sandwiches, carrot sticks, and apple slices. Spread a checked tablecloth over a child-size table and invite everyone to bring their favorite stuffed animal for a backyard lunch.

Did You Know?

♦ The English word "picnic" was first mentioned in a letter written by Lord Chesterfield in the 1740s.

♦ Picnics probably began as moveable outdoor feasts, such as medieval hunting feasts.

♦ Wealthy Washingtonians expecting an easy Union victory took a picnic lunch to view the Battle of Bull Run.

♦ Picnics are often described in literature of the Victorian era.

♦ Painters such as Claude Monet, Auguste Renoir, and Paul Cèzanne used a picnic theme in some of their paintings.

♦ Picnics were originally thought to be potluck with contributions from all who attended. By the 1860s, a picnic came to mean eating outdoors.

♦ In 2000, France celebrated the first Bastille Day of the new millennium with a 600-mile-long picnic.

♦ The Fourth of July is one of the most popular days in the United States for having a picnic.

Why not enjoy the cool of the morning and start the day with a breakfast picnic—complete with biscuits filled with eggs, cheese, bacon, sausage, country ham, or jelly? Serve glasses of fresh-squeezed orange juice as you greet the morning sun. What better way to get a fun-filled weekend adventure started?

And picnics don't have to be limited to summertime. You can toast the harvest moon with warm mugs of apple cider and freshly baked cookies while stargazing. Or enjoy a winter picnic with hot chocolate and fixings on a cozy blanket (over a waterproof tarp) spread out on a snowy bank or in front of a campfire.

Way to Go!

Don't let bad weather douse your picnic plans. Spread a colorful quilt in the middle of the living room floor and have a picnic with all the trimmings. Create ambience for your indoor picnic. Play a nature tape and turn on the ceiling fan—or pretend there's a warm summer breeze. If it's a winter picnic you want, bring all the fixings and sit on a blanket in front of a roaring fireplace.

Picnics can be a quick getaway to brighten a day, a celebration for a special occasion or holiday, a fun excuse to make a trip to the park, nearby forest, or music festival—or include a picnic with one of the other backyard activities mentioned in this book and make it a real adventure.

Think of your little corner of the world—your backyard—as a place of adventure, fun, and discovery. Explore your backyard as if you have never been there before. Think creatively. Share the fun.

Chapter 3

Training Camp

In This Chapter

- ◆ Exploring sports camps
- ◆ Making a big splash with a swimming adventure
- ◆ It's a balancing act on boards and blades
- ◆ "Look, Mom … no hands!": bicycling
- ◆ Will that be a 5K or a marathon?
- ◆ From checkmate to sudoku

For sports stars and enthusiasts alike, training camp is a large part of their success. Whatever the sport—NFL or collegiate football, baseball, basketball, or soccer—they all participate in hundreds of hours of training individually and with their teams. Olympic contenders train both on their own and in various training camps. There is spring training for college football, cheerleading, and other competitions. In the winter, baseball teams head south to camps in warmer climes. Whatever sport you choose to participate in, you have to practice, practice, and practice in order to become good.

Training and practice is not limited to just physical sports, however. Individuals and teams involved in games of intellect, knowledge, and even chance train, too. Monopoly, Scrabble, Trivial Pursuit, and crossword puzzle enthusiasts need to constantly train and practice both on an individual basis and with a team or group. This continuous training prepares them for various competitions within their interest.

A training camp adventure for your family is a great way to learn a new sport or game, participate in favorite sports with family members, and have a great time sharing the fun!

See Appendix A for suggested books and websites relating to the activities in this chapter.

Sport Camps

Many large universities offer summer camp for baseball, basketball, football, cheerleading, soccer, and other competitive sports. Granted, these can be expensive—but if you are attending a local camp, you will eliminate travel expenses and may be able to stay at home. You will want to research whether there are any collegiate camps available in your locale. One less-expensive alternative is attending a camp or training offered at your local community college, high school, or parks and recreation department. Local camps give you the opportunity to learn by watching and/or participating. Start by attending practice sessions and talking to participants, which will give you an idea of whether this sport may interest individual family members or your entire family. Attending these kinds of events is a fun activity for the entire family as spectators. And while you are enjoying the game, you are learning—the rules, the finesse, and the strategy of winning.

What You'll Need

   ♦ Brochures and information about sport camps in your area
   ♦ Rule book(s)

If one of your family members decides on a sports adventure, be sure to check with your family doctor before beginning a new sport. You also want to find out what type of preliminary warm up stretching and strengthening exercises are necessary before you begin training for any new sports adventure.

Do your homework, learn the rules of the game, and make sure that you understand the scoring system and the terms used in the sport. You may want to catch a few competitions or practice sessions at the local stadium or park or watch a match on TV. Invite an enthusiast or player over for dinner and a tutorial session about the sport.

Did You Know?

♦ Baseball's home plate is 17 inches wide.

♦ A regulation football field is 360 feet long and 160 feet wide.

♦ The first New York City marathon was held in 1970 with a total of 127 runners. In 2006, 38,000 runners crossed the finish line.

♦ An estimated $800 million worth of golf balls are used by golfers annually.

♦ Fourteen feathers is the allowed number of feathers for a badminton bird according to official Olympic rules.

♦ In 1930, Uruguay held the first soccer World Cup.

♦ In 1891, physical education teacher James Naismith set out to invent a game to occupy students between football and baseball seasons. That game was basketball.

♦ In baseball, a perfect game is one in which the same pitcher pitches the entire game without allowing any player on the opposing team to reach first base.

If it's basketball that catches your interest, look for pickup games in your neighborhood or at a nearby school yard or park. Or you may already have a basketball hoop. Spend time practicing free throws. Take turns dribbling and playing catch. Keep a dated chart of the number of attempted baskets and the number of baskets. Compare your statistics over a period of time (a week, a month).

If it's baseball you like, find an open field or go to a batting cage and practice hitting baseballs or softballs. Learn to use a mitt when playing catch in the backyard. Gather family, friends, classmates, and neighbors for a game in a nearby vacant lot. Or go to a park where fields are available. I've only mentioned basketball and baseball, but whatever sport you are interested in—football, cheerleading, tennis, soccer—there is sure to be a training camp you can attend or teams that you can join. And you can always create your own camp.

Always remember, though, that you are playing the game for fun. A little competition can add to the fun, but make sure that it's *friendly* competition.

Easy Does It

Be sure to check with your family doctor before beginning any new exercise routine or sport.

Design a training camp around your family's interests. If someone in the family can't provide the coaching, locate an expert or contact a "star" of the game who lives in your town or neighborhood. Ask whether that person would be willing to spend a day or two—or maybe a few hours over several weeks—at your house, teaching your family the sport. You can also get together with friends and neighbors to create your own camp, drawing from each person's expertise and sharing your own.

In order to include everyone in the fun, be sure to simplify it for younger children—helping them get the gist of the game. Older children will be ready to learn some of the rules, and of course the teenage group should already have a good grasp on the basics, scoring, and strategy of winning. Keep records for each child of the number of baskets attempted and the number made, the longest shot, and so on—and do the same for baseball (the number of attempts hitting the ball and number of hits, the longest distance the ball is hit, and so on). Each sport has different kinds of statistics. Keeping these records will help kids see how much they have learned and improved over time. Plus, the child competes against himself or herself rather than against someone else.

Many sports can get expensive because of the equipment needed (for playing and safety). If you are just trying out a new sport, look for used equipment. Garage sales, thrift shops, and secondhand sporting goods stores are excellent resources.

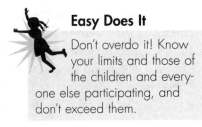

Easy Does It

Don't overdo it! Know your limits and those of the children and everyone else participating, and don't exceed them.

Training camp is a great way to try several sports or become proficient in one. Just be sure to make it fun—sharing time, learning something new, and the exhilaration of the sport.

Big Splash

With the heat of summer comes thoughts of having fun in cool water. Paddling around in the pool or floating along on an ocean wave are both wonderful ideas. Whether your family is going to the pool or the beach, it's imperative that everyone can swim. And it's even better if you and your family members are good swimmers. Many swimmers never learn the proper strokes or lifesaving techniques; both are important for having a safe and fun water adventure. Make a big splash with a swimming adventure that encourages all family members to work on their swimming and lifesaving skills while having a great time in the water.

What You'll Need

- ◆ List of public pools
- ◆ Swim lesson schedules
- ◆ Swim suits
- ◆ Swim vests

If your family members do not swim or you have young children, by all means take swim lessons. Many YMCAs and parks and recreation departments offer swim classes and lifeguard certification. Check to see whether you have a local organization that offers swim lessons that are appropriate for the entire family. If your family plans to participate together, you may want to see whether you can hire a certified instructor for a few private lessons and then encourage each age group to participate in some group lessons with their peers. A little peer pressure may encourage some reluctant children to join in. And soon, you will have your entire family ready for a great swim adventure!

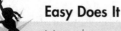

Easy Does It

Never leave a child alone or unattended near the water. Use the buddy system at the pool or beach.

For those in the family who already know how to swim, a big splash adventure is a good time to brush up on their skills or learn new strokes, such as the breaststroke or the butterfly. It may also be a great time to become certified as a lifeguard. Not only will it benefit them, but it also means the possibility of working at a pool or beach.

As you are learning various swim strokes, play follow-the-leader, practicing the most recently learned swim strokes. It will help everyone become more familiar with the strokes and encourage practicing while having a great time.

Learning to swim laps not only can be enjoyable but also can serve as great exercise and an introduction to racing. Kids always love good, friendly competition. They will improve their swimming skills and exercise at the same time. Of course, competition doesn't always have to be against someone else. Swimming is a sport where you can compete against yourself. Keep records of your time and number of laps. After a week or two, you can see how far you've come. You may then want to begin setting goals of swimming a certain number of laps in a specified amount of time. Be creative; challenge yourself and other members of your family.

Last but not least, what about synchronized swimming? Get together and choreograph your own synchronized swim team. Put on a show and have someone take a video for you to watch on a cold, snowy day next winter. Be safe, have fun, be silly, and enjoy the water.

Did You Know?

◆ 2500 B.C.E.—Swimming is depicted in Egyptian hiero-
glyphics.

◆ 400 B.C.E.—Egyptians and Romans leisurely dove off
cliffs.

◆ 78 C.E.—Romans introduced swimming to Britain.

◆ Fourteenth century—Medieval knights mastered swimming in armor.

◆ Eighteenth century—Swimming in the sea was popular-
ized by George III.

◆ Nineteenth century—Germany and Sweden developed acrobatic diving.

◆ 1845—The first swimming championship debuted in
Sydney, Australia.

◆ 1875—The first documented swim across the English
Channel was completed by Captain Webb.

◆ 1885—The first diving competition was held in Germany.

◆ 1892—The first swim championship for women was
held in Scotland.

◆ 1924—Johnny Weissmuller set 67 world records in
swimming before starring in the *Tarzan* movies.

Boards and Blades

Surfboards, skateboards, snowboards, roller skates, and inline skates
are everywhere. Most of the time, it all looks so easy and fun—but it's
not nearly as easy as it looks. Not only do these sports require a lot of
practice, but you also need to be in great physical condition, use well-
maintained equipment, and wear the proper safety gear. You should be
cautious. Get instruction, because these sports can be dangerous for a
novice.

What You'll Need

◆ Boards and/or skates

◆ Proper safety equipment for the sport you choose

◆ A safe place to practice

Find out where the locals go to surf, skate, or snowboard. Take time to watch the activities. Ask questions about equipment, trainers and training, and safety issues. Learn the lingo associated with the sport as well as any protocols.

For a fun activity, invite the neighborhood stars over for lunch or along on an outing. Have them do a demonstration or set up training sessions. Kids usually won't pass up a free meal, and they'll love showing off their tricks. They can brag about their best rides, talk about their worst falls, and provide you and your children with some real insight into what it takes to ride a board or to skate. Ask them to show you the basics. You definitely want to talk about safety issues and find out about the best riding and safety equipment. Find out what is needed for maintaining equipment. You don't want your inline skates to lock up just as you start down a long hill. Plan several training and practice sessions. You can also pick up some videos or watch the sports on television.

Balance is key to these activities. The easiest avenue may be to spend some Saturday afternoons at the local skating rink. A pair of roller skates will get you started learning to balance on wheels. This is especially a good way to get younger kids involved. Once they get to the point where they can skate around the circle without falling down, introduce an obstacle course to challenge their control and balance. Then, add some friendly competition with racing around the obstacle course. They'll have fun while also gaining strength and skills for moving on to inline skating. Inline skates require new skills and different balance because they have only one set of wheels.

Easy Does It

Some public places don't allow skating or skateboarding. If "no skaters allowed" signs are posted or there are rules against skating or skateboarding in an area, don't do it!

From roller skates to inline skating, once you have the balance down, you may want to try out a skateboard. If there is a skate park or arena in your area, that is a good place to go for pointers and practice. You may also be able to use your driveway, the sidewalk, a paved school yard, or a quiet parking lot. Wherever you practice, just make sure that it's safe and away from traffic and pedestrians.

During the off season, surfers often train on skateboards. In fact, surfers first started the sport of skateboarding. Balance is again very important in both sports as well as in snowboarding. Riding skateboards and especially the large-carve boards will help you finesse your turning and weaving from side to side—in much the same way as you would ride a wave.

Did You Know?

◆ The Hawaiian word for surfing is *he'e nalu.*

◆ In the 1800s, the Dutch used wooden wheels on their ice skates so they could skate in the summer.

◆ The first national snowboard race was held in 1982 in Woodstock, Vermont.

◆ In 1908, Madison Square Garden in New York City was used as a roller skating rink.

◆ During the 1970s and 1980s, more than 4,000 roller-discos were in operation.

◆ Inline skates usually have four or five wheels arranged in a single line.

◆ Skateboarding or "sidewalk surfing" originated in the 1950s.

Both surfing and snowboarding are limited by locale and climate, but one can always dream and practice with the hope of getting to go for it. When the opportunity does arrive, be sure to take advantage of camps and lessons available. Learning from and working with an expert will make the adventure much safer and more fun. And if you think that you have an interest in surfing, you should probably perfect your swimming first. One backyard adventure can easily prepare you for another!

All of this equipment can get expensive—especially if the entire family is involved. Again, save money and spend a weekend checking out garage sales, thrift shops, and secondhand sporting goods stores for inexpensive equipment to get your family started on a boards and blades adventure.

Ride with the Wind

Biking, cycling, bicycle riding—whatever you call it, riding a bicycle can be exhilarating, provide excellent exercise, and prove to be a wonderful, inexpensive mode of transportation. With the introduction of the rumble seat trailer, the entire family can tag along on a bike ride.

What You'll Need

- Bicycles appropriate for the age and size of your children
- Adult bicycles
- Proper safety helmets

If your baby started tagging along in a rumble seat, he or she will soon want to join the family fun. Initially, it may mean short rides around the neighborhood with a tricycle following behind. As size and age permit, young children can move up to bicycles with training wheels and maybe add another block or two to their ride. The entire family will celebrate on that glorious day: "Look, Mom … no training wheels!" At last, it can truly be a family outing.

Now that your children can ride alone, you will want to perfect their skills. Set up an obstacle course for them to ride through. Have them practice turning corners, left and right, as well as starting and stopping. When the kids are ready to ride alone, begin extending those neighborhood excursions or take bike paths and trails through parks and other public areas where there is no motorized traffic. Plan short weekend rides with a destination in mind, such as the playground, the ice cream shop, a pizza parlor, or to visit grandparents, nearby friends, or neighbors. Cycling together as a family can become a routine weekend event. As children become more proficient, you may want to pack a lunch and make it a true family cycling adventure.

While learning the basic techniques and skills for riding, you will also want to be sure that safety precautions and the rules of the road are part of the education. Four important rules to remember are:

- Always wear a helmet—you never know when you might take a nasty fall.

- Ride on the right side of the road with traffic.

- Use appropriate hand signals to indicate that you're making a turn.

- Follow traffic signals (for example, stop at a red light).

Bicycles, protective gear, and accessories can get expensive. So while you are out exploring on your bikes, you may want to peruse garage sales, flea markets, thrift stores, and secondhand sporting goods stores for used equipment in good condition.

Let your children help plan the family's weekend tour by helping chart a course. As incentive and for fun, add family competition or individual goal setting, keeping records of distances, number of loops around the playground or park, or days riding. And don't forget the practical side of riding to the neighborhood grocery for a carton of milk or a loaf of bread. If you live close enough, you may want to get in the habit of riding to and from school with your student. And if you are lucky enough to have grandparents nearby, you can get in the habit of riding over for a short visit. Want to bet that Grandma will bake cookies when she knows that you're coming?

Way to Go!

Did you know that less than 50 percent of United States car trips are fewer than 2 miles, but only 1 percent of trips in this country are made by bicycle? Save on gas and get in shape at the same time! Get in the habit of riding your bike for nearby errands.

Did You Know?

◆ "Bicycle" as a vehicle name dates back to 1869.

◆ The chain is composed of half of all the parts in a typical bicycle.

◆ Equal size wheels, hollow steel tubing, coaster brakes, and adjustable handlebars identify the safety bicycle, which was universally adopted by manufacturers in the United States in the 1880s.

◆ There are almost 400 million bicycles in China and about one billion bicycles worldwide.

◆ Bicycles used air-filled tires before automobiles did.

◆ In 1969, about half of all students walked or bicycled to school.

Inquire about family cycling clubs in the area—or start your own. You can invite neighbors, family, and friends to join the fun. Plan a special outing in May to celebrate American Bike Month. As skill increases, some members of the family may decide they want to participate in local competitions and riding events.

Cycling is an excellent exercise, promotes goods health, offers alternative transportation, and is a fun family backyard adventure.

Off to the Races

Make running a family affair. Running—like cycling—can be enjoyed by everyone in the family, young and old alike. Many new strollers are made especially for runners and joggers, making it easy to take little ones along. And even grandparents may be runners. The family will want to set a pace that accommodates all members of the group.

School-age children may be required to run in their physical education classes. And most often, they are exposed to track and cross-country running and relay races through school track meets. Plan to attend after-school practices and track meets. Get to know the track coach and local running pros. You may want to watch local community runs to see how easy or hard it can be to participate in competitive runs. Attending a local run is also another good opportunity to meet other families who are interested in the sport.

What You'll Need

- ◆ Running shoes
- ◆ Appropriate clothing
- ◆ A stopwatch (optional)

As a family, you can set goals, plan courses, and train for upcoming meets. Each individual can keep a running log and record his or her own personal best time—competing with themselves as well as striving to achieve established group goals. Together as a family, you decide where the route will lead you. At first, you will probably want to do short runs with little or no incline—but as you practice together, you will want to increase the distance and add a few short hills along the way.

Just for fun, find out what the local and world records are for each type of race for both men and women. As your family gets more competitive, you may want to set the distance and use a stopwatch to see how close or far you are from local and world records. Keeping time and distance statistics will also help each member of the family to see just how far he or she has advanced.

Easy Does It

Invest in the proper footwear. Wearing the wrong shoes can not only cause blisters but also problems with your knees and back.

Did You Know?

♦ A 5K run is equal to 3.2 miles.

♦ A 10K run is equal to 6.2 miles.

♦ A marathon is 26.2 miles.

♦ Most tracks are oval and 400 meters in length (1,312 feet or just under a quarter-mile).

♦ The only road-racing distance run in major international athletics championships such as the Olympics is the marathon.

♦ Track and field athletics in the United States dates from the 1860s.

♦ The first Boston marathon was run in 1897.

Find out about local charity runs and walks. At first, you may want to observe and get acquainted with other like-minded people. If you think you want to compete in a group, begin by choosing a low-key walk or running competition. You will find others who decide to walk the entire distance to finish the course. Depending on family interest and abilities, you may find you want to encourage other families to join you. Or you may want to find local running clubs to join for that added incentive or inspiration. If you or a family member really gets involved in running, look for a group that trains for marathons. Join them on their regular training sessions. At first, if may be hard to keep up—but with regular practice, you will improve. A group like this will have a number of seasoned runners who are willing to offer tips and suggestions for making your running fun and easy. In addition, many of these groups often train together and then travel to compete in marathons nationally and worldwide.

Game Time

When we think of training camp, we, of course, assume we are training for a physical sport. But it doesn't have to be. Why not train for a mental competition? There are spelling bees, geography competitions, and other school-related events. But what about board games, puzzles, or cards? Your family may be interested in mental competitions—perhaps board games such as Scrabble, Monopoly, checkers and chess, or Trivial Pursuit. Or you all may play card games such as bridge, pinochle, canasta, and poker. Do you enjoy working jigsaw puzzles or squaring off with crossword puzzles or sudoku? And then there is the ancient game of dominoes with its many game-playing variations. And it may be that your family already has a favorite game or pastime that isn't mentioned here but still fits the bill. As always, you will want to choose a game that the entire family can enjoy, so this may mean starting with checkers, Old Maid, or Chutes and Ladders and working your way up to Monopoly or Trivial Pursuit. Decide which game (or games) your family aspires to master.

What You'll Need

◆ Games, cards, and/or puzzles

◆ A card table or space for playing

◆ Rule book(s)

◆ A paper and pencil for scoring

Competition is just as stiff in the mental arena as it is in sports—and to be a great competitor, you need to know the rules and etiquette of the competition. You will also want to learn about strategy and finesse—and, as with sports, you will need to practice.

Try several games. Have a little friendly family competition. Set up your own marathon of board games. See how many times you can play and win the same board game or how many different board games you can play during a weekend. If it's an extended family adventure, set up several tables with one game or a variety of games, and move from table to table. Have an all-night Scrabble or Monopoly party. As the skill increases, you may want to compete with friends and neighbors. Look for groups in your area that meet at the local coffee shop, park, or someone's house to play on any given night. Find out what it takes to join the group, or form your own group. There are several sites online where you can compete with other like-minded gamers or set up friendly family games; see Appendix A for a sampling. You can even play Scrabble via e-mail.

Why not have a family trivia night? Initially, you may want to adapt the game to the appropriate age group and build on the difficulty of the questions. You could even spend family time making up your own family trivia cards related to family members and events. What a great way for little ones to practice learning telephone numbers, street addresses, or colors! As your family members get older, the questions can increase in difficulty. If you're not into making your own game, look for an age-appropriate trivia game. Trivia comes in all sorts of knowledge, interest, and age ranges. You can have great fun as well as provide a real learning experience.

If card games are the family's choice, make sure you have an official book of rules for the game(s) you play. Keep it fair and fun, making sure that everyone understands and plays by the rules. As you gain knowledge of the game, you will want to learn the strategy and finesse that ultimately wins the game. Cards are portable, and you can most often use the same deck for a variety of different games—from Old Maid to bridge. Take them with you on a family picnic outing, and after a scrumptious picnic adventure, lull in the shade of a tree and play a few rounds of cards. Or pull out the cards and get some competition going on a snowy day when there is "nothing" to do.

Have an ongoing jigsaw puzzle adventure. Keep one or two puzzles set up on tables throughout the house, stopping to place a piece as you walk by. For a little family competition, set up tables with the same puzzle or puzzles with the same number of pieces and see who can work theirs the quickest. Work the puzzle upside down. True, you don't get to see the picture as you are working—but you do learn to differentiate the shapes of the pieces and how they fit together. You can also purchase puzzles that have pictures on both sides, thus making it more difficult to fit the pieces together. Another puzzler for jigsaw puzzles is to mix two or three sets of puzzle pieces together and work all three puzzles at the same time. That'll keep everyone busy trying to figure out which piece goes in which puzzle. Jigsaw puzzles come in all shapes and sizes, from one-piece wooden puzzles for tiny hands to large, complicated, three-dimensional creations.

Did You Know?

◆ Monopoly is the best-selling board game in the world. The longest Monopoly game on record lasted 70 straight days.

◆ Scrabble can be found in one out of every three American homes. More than 175 Scrabble tournaments are held each year in North America.

◆ Crossword puzzles are popular throughout the world. The first known published crossword puzzle was introduced on December 21, 1913, in the Sunday newspaper *New York World.*

◆ Trivial Pursuit was introduced to the United States at the American International Toy Fair in New York City in February 1982.

◆ Chess is played by millions of people worldwide in clubs, online, by correspondence, and in tournaments. Chess has its origin in Indian games. The current form of the game emerged in southern Europe in the late fifteenth century.

◆ Commercial jigsaw puzzles originated in London in 1760. The biggest commercially available jigsaw puzzle is 24,000 pieces.

◆ The earliest playing cards are believed to have originated in Central Asia. The designs on playing cards are derived from designs used by the French.

◆ Dominoes evolved from dice. The standard double-six domino set represents all the rolls of two six-sided dice. The oldest known domino set is dated from around 1120 C.E.

◆ Sudoku means "single number" in Japanese. Sudoku was first published in the United States in 1979 as "Number Place."

Way to Go!

If younger children are not ready for crossword puzzles or sudoku, give them the puzzles and some crayons or markers to fill in the blank spaces. While the adults and big kids work their own puzzles, the little ones can create a work of art.

Crossword puzzles or sudoku can be worked together, or make copies for each family member and compete to see who can finish the puzzle first. And like cards and crossword puzzles, sudoku is portable. Take these games with you on other outings, such as a picnic or camping adventure, for a quiet activity.

The entire family can play dominoes. You can start with the picture ones made especially for smaller children. As they learn their numbers, you can move on to the real deal. There are many variations in game play—the most common being matching the number of dots on the tiles and scoring accordingly. With its long history and many variations, you are sure to find a domino game that's perfect for your family fun.

Yes, you can train for chess, Scrabble, bridge, or crossword puzzle tournaments. As your family's skills improve, you may want to find local competitions. Locate a chess club, find out who the best bridge players are, locate a trivia group, or inquire about the requirements for qualifying to compete in crossword puzzle contests. Often, you can find a group that plays one of the games regularly at a local coffee shop or at the park. Find out whether there are any competitions in your area and attend them. Learn who the experts are, and ask for tips. You will have lots of family fun with a game-time adventure.

Training camp requires work and dedication from participants but may result in a lifelong interest. Dive in and enjoy the competition, whether you choose a physical sport or mental competition. Your family is sure to experience great adventures at training camp!

Chapter 4

Trading Places

In This Chapter

- Being Mom and Dad for the day
- Discovering cultural differences at home
- Another time, another place
- There's more to work than meets the eye
- Have fun helping others

At one time or another, all of us wish we were someone else or somewhere else. One of the ways we fulfill that wish is by spending our vacation time exploring other lifestyles and environments. When we're on vacation, we are more open to doing new and different things—breaking the routine of our everyday life. Vacations can also be a time for inner reflection and exploration. You may find a new freedom or experience a revelation when you have an opportunity to walk in someone else's shoes and experience other lifestyles and settings.

So ... why not try on some other shoes by trading places? Take turns being Mom or Dad for the day, enjoying the privileges of adulthood as well as the responsibility of taking care of your family (and just being boss!). Explore other cultures through food, music, and folk stories. Relive the past (a day without television, computers, and iPods) or imagine the future as you would create it. Experience the world of work beyond the nine to five and discover how it influences daily lifestyles from dinner time to weekend activities. Or you can lend a hand, volunteering your time and energy to benefit a cause dear to your heart.

Trading places can be a fun and rewarding adventure, but it requires commitment, energy, and a willingness from the entire family to participate.

See Appendix A for suggested books and websites relating to the activities in this chapter.

No Place Like Home

Having your kids become Mom or Dad for the day can be a real eye-opener for kids and parents alike. With busy work and school schedules, there is sometimes little time to think about how we act and react to daily joys and disappointments. It may be hard to see how our actions and interactions affect other members of the family. Role playing helps kids understand the reasons behind the rules and gives parents an inside view of how they look or sound to their children. This is certainly a great way to open up dialog that may not have occurred without role playing. This all sounds so serious, but it can be great fun. How many dads would love to try out a new skateboard—but having to be responsible has kept him from indulging in some fun?

What You'll Need

- ◆ A family meeting to discuss and agree on guidelines and boundaries

After your family has agreed on the details of the trade, choose a day or a weekend where the kids will be Mom and Dad and parents get to be the kids. Be sure to set strict guidelines as to the time period when you will be trading places. You will also want to have a "deal breaker" agreement if something should happen that requires Mom or Dad to step back into their supervisory roles. It could be an irresolvable squabble between siblings or someone having an accident and requiring adult attention. Once the guidelines, boundaries, and "deal breaker" agreement are established, you are ready to set a time.

The guidelines and boundaries, of course, mean doing chores and abiding by the family's rules, including eating all your vegetables and going to bed on time. Hear that, Mom and Dad? And consequently, kids may need to grocery shop, rake leaves, do

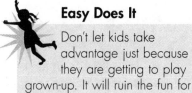

Easy Does It

Don't let kids take advantage just because they are getting to play grown-up. It will ruin the fun for everyone.

the laundry, prepare nutritious meals and clean up the kitchen, clean house, and wash the car. Parents, there's also that opportunity to curl up in your favorite corner and read, go for a bike ride, work a puzzle, play games, or play with the dog. The kids will love having control of the TV remote, dictating bedtimes, or deciding what Mom or Dad are going to wear that day.

As I mentioned, you will want to lay down some guidelines and consider safety issues before committing to trading places. The ability to trade places will also depend on the age of the children. For very young ones, you may want to trade with only one parent on one day and with the other the next time. That way, there is some parental guidance but still the opportunity to experience trading places. With older children, it can be a good learning tool as it prepares them for some of the problems of living on their own once college rolls around.

Get started by making a list of family chores, which may include setting and clearing the table, taking out the trash, making your bed, and walking the dog. Also make a list of family fun—things that parents do that the kids would love—such as staying up late and watching TV. Making this work both from the standpoint of fun and learning about each other requires everyone to go with the flow and enjoy the tradeoff—knowing it is all in good fun. Keep an open mind. A child's viewpoint may give everyone a different perspective on certain rules.

Did You Know?

◆ A baby goes through about 7,300 diapers by the time he or she turns two years old.

◆ A family averages 330 loads of laundry per year.

◆ The first Mother's Day was celebrated in 1908.

◆ The first Father's Day was celebrated in 1910.

◆ The U.S. Census for the year 2000 reported that the average family size is 3.14.

Of course, trading places doesn't have to mean just parents and children. Trading places with friends can be a real adventure. Family friends and neighborhoods might want to take turns keeping all the kids so that Mom and Dad can have time alone. This is an especially good opportunity for the only child to experience life with siblings or gives a sibling an opportunity to be the only child. Because there are always different rules, routines, and reprimands in each family, it's also interesting for children to see how similar problems are resolved in different families—a lesson in socializing within the constraint of new surroundings and rules. It's an opportunity to be exposed to different foods, music, traditions, and family relationships. It gives everyone an opportunity to learn and grow while having fun.

If you do an exchange with another family, when you get back together as a family it may be fun to compare family rules, expectations, and rewards. Before doing the exchange, make a list of 10 or more commonly accepted rules at your house, such as bedtime, chores, and dinner etiquette. Some examples are as follows: everyone is expected to be at the dinner table on time; the last person to leave the room turns out the light; pockets must be emptied before putting clothes into the laundry basket; and so on. Compare your family's rules with your exchange family's rules to see how they correspond. It might even be a good time to negotiate and incorporate new rules, expectations, and rewards.

Remember—before trading places either with Mom and Dad or another family—set up some guidelines. Staying within prescribed boundaries will prevent misunderstandings and hurt feelings. Make this a fun learning adventure well worth remembering.

Culture Shock

Our previous adventure touches on the possibility of different families having different rules and customs. That can be true whether they've always lived in the same town as your family or in another part of the country or world. Often, family rules and customs are handed down from generation to generation—and no one knows for sure how they started. It was just the way Grandmother did it or what Grandpa expected. Most often, you find these kinds of rules and customs associated with celebrations and meals. It's fun to learn about new rules and customs. You may discover one or two that you want to add to your family's traditions.

Of course, if you take a new look at your rules and customs, you may find some that have been handed down that make no sense in your family. I started one without realizing it. When my children were young and eggshell crafts were popular, I would always put the broken eggshell back in the carton—my way of saving the shells when I was busy cooking. One day while visiting my daughter, my son-in-law was questioning why she always put the shells back in the carton—saying that it made no sense. But she had picked up the habit from me without knowing the reasoning behind it. So, you see that rules and customs don't necessarily come from a long cultural tradition or even make sense.

For starters, you may want to explore different rules and customs with close friends, neighbors, or other family members. And it may be that you want to think about some of the customs your family adheres to, especially when it comes to celebrating holidays, birthdays, or sharing a Sunday dinner. As you discover these small differences, consider looking farther to other regions of the country or world.

What You'll Need

- Books, videos, brochures, and maps of the region you choose
- Friends or neighbors from the region (optional)

Due to issues of safety and the prohibitive cost of travel for families these days, it's difficult to explore new lifestyles in faraway places. An alternative to traveling abroad is to bring other cultures to you. You can explore other cultures, countries, or regions of your own country. Food, song, dance, dress, and storytelling are great ways to experience and learn about another culture. Pick a country or region that is of interest to the whole family and research it.

Whether your family decides to explore locally, another region of the United States, or another country, the best place to start your research is at the public library. Pick up books about the region's history, celebrations, religions, dress, crafts, foods, and traditions.

If your family has chosen another part of the country, learn colloquialisms for that region. Buy newspapers or magazines from the chosen area at your local news stand or bookstore. What events are listed? What is the favorite pastime? Check out the video store for movies and documentaries about the region. Find out about the schools. Find out what is similar and different about another area of the country. Depending on the time it was settled, it may have a different viewpoint of American history. What are the stories of that region? Who lived there and when? Plan meals unique to that locale, share favorite children's stories, and learn songs. Post a map on the wall and locate the major cities, rivers, mountain ranges, and large bodies of water. What kind of climate does the region have? Learn about the plant and animal life. All of these areas give insight into how and why a culture developed as it has.

Way to Go!

Families with school-age children can divide the research up into different areas and appropriate age levels, letting each member of the family contribute.

If you choose another country, you can use many of the same suggestions. Find out what the predominant religion is. What is the type of government? How long has it been in power? You may also want to locate cultural centers or churches associated with the country. Attend festivals and cultural events, and get acquainted with the country and its people. Plan a traditional birthday celebration or celebrate a holiday associated with the area. You may find something new to add to your family's traditional celebrations.

Did You Know?

◆ In Brazil, the birthday child receives a pull on the ear-
   lobe for each year.

◆ In Denmark, a flag is flown outside a window to let
   everyone know someone is having a birthday.

◆ In Holland, a child receives an especially large gift on
   a crown-year birthday (when the child turns 5, 10, 15,
   20, and 21).

◆ In Hungary, the birthday child takes candy to school
   to give to classmates.

◆ In Israel, the birthday child sits in a chair while grownups raise and lower the chair for each year of the
   child's age—plus one for good luck.

◆ In Mexico, the birthday child is blindfolded and hits
   a piñata. When it's broken open, the goodies are
   shared with all the children present.

◆ In Russia, birthday pies are served instead of birthday
   cakes.

◆ In Vietnam, everyone's birthday is celebrated on New
   Year's Day.

Look through the ethnic food aisles of your local supermarket or find
out whether there are ethnic markets in your area that carry foods indig-
enous to the region you are exploring. Are there any restaurants in your
area that specialize in the food from that region of the country or the
world? Discover what foods you are familiar with that may have come
from that area. If the language is different, learn to say please and thank
you, hello and goodbye in the region's language. Dress today has become
fairly generic worldwide, but you can research the traditional dress used
for special occasions in that country. You may want to learn about traditional celebrations—birthdays, weddings, and other commemorative
events. If you are lucky enough to have someone in your town from that
country or region, you might invite him or her to show and tell. What
better way to make new friends and learn about our world?

You don't have to leave home to explore other regions of the country or the world. Learn about other customs, foods, and celebrations. Create your own cultural adventure, and bring the world to your own backyard.

Time Travel

A trip to Williamsburg, Virginia; Old Salem, Massachusetts; or other historical sites gives us a look at life in America's early settlements. Visiting these places only gives us a superficial view of how life really was. Actually living the life is a far greater learning experience. Pick a period in history—and it doesn't have to be early Americana. Just going back to the 1950s could be a real eye-opener for today's children and many of their parents. The 1950s was an era before computers, video games, and microwave ovens. Imagine no TV or only a small black-and-white television. Listen to the music from that era, enjoy a TV dinner, and watch old reruns of *Father Knows Best, Leave It to Beaver,* or *I Love Lucy.* For families with older children, you may want to discuss the political climate and the Cold War—all an important part of the 1950s and American history.

If the 1950s are too recent, choose another period—perhaps before radios, telephones, electricity, or indoor plumbing. How does one take a bath, cook, or read without electricity? What's for dinner, and where do you find it? What did children and adults do for entertainment? What did people wear and why? These are all wonderful questions to ask about the past or the future. Yes, I said "future"—who said that you have to go *back* in time? What will you eat, where will you live, and how will you travel from one place to the next? Imagine clothing styles, hairdos, and food in the future. Be visionaries and predict the future 10, 20, or even 50 years from now. Let your imagination run wild!

What You'll Need

+ Books, videos, and DVDs about the chosen period

+ Drawing paper and pencils, crayons, and markers

If it's an adventure into the past that your family craves, head to the library to get books about that period. Learn the history; look at the style of dress, modes of transportation, and political climate. Watch documentaries of that era. Many areas of the country have reenactments, plays, and festivals related to the Renaissance, colonial America, or life during the Civil War. If there's one in your town, by all means attend. What music was popular? What games were being played? Are there favorite children's stories from that era? Once you have learned about the time you plan to travel to, consider how you currently accomplish your everyday chores. Then, think about how you will accomplish those tasks without some of today's work-saving appliances, convenience foods, and multitude of shopping venues. Will you have to draw water from the well to do the dishes? Will you have to cook on the stove or in the oven instead of popping a treat into the microwave? Will you listen to radio shows instead of watching television?

Did You Know?

♦ In 1890, running water was considered a luxury.

♦ In 1920, only 1 percent of households had central heat.

♦ Only half of the households in 1950 owned a vacuum cleaner or washing machine.

♦ Television was introduced to American households in the early 1950s.

♦ Microwave ovens became the norm in the 1980s.

♦ Computers, the Internet, cell phones, CDs, and DVD players became commonplace in the 1990s.

You may want to start with the near and dear past—when Mom and Dad were kids. What was a day like back then? What time did they have to get up to be ready for school? How did they get to school? What was their favorite pastime, game, or television show(s)? Watch some of the old shows and play a game or two. What was their favorite food? Is it still their favorite food? What better way to get to know more about Mom and Dad than to reminisce and reenact their childhood days. Look through old photo albums; maybe Mom still has a dress or two from when she was in high school, so try it on to see how it fits. What books were they reading? Did Dad play sports? Does he still have a jersey that he wore? Try it on. Talk about how sports are similar and different now.

If there are lots of old photos and memorabilia from days gone by, you may want to work together as a family to preserve them in scrapbooks. Work together to sort through old photos, concert ticket stubs, birthday cards, and other mementos. Share the experiences as you preserve the memorabilia in scrapbooks, getting Mom or Dad to relate stories associated with these special items. Record tidbits of information with each item in the book, or you may want to do an oral history—recording the story on tape.

Once Mom and Dad's childhood history is recorded, begin similar books for each child. Pick out photos and talk about when and why they were taken. Record some special tidbits about the pictures. Children may want to add some of their drawings or write a story about themselves. What better way to get to know each other as a family?

Don't forget the grandparents. What a wealth of information they have to share. Ask them what was going on in the world when they were young. Compare how their lives are the same and different from those of kids today. Listen to some of the music; look for books that were popular when they were young. Learn the dances of that era. What did they wear? Do they still have any clothes they saved from when they were teenagers? Did they have chores? Ask about family rules and traditions, like bedtime, Sunday dinner, and family outings.

Way to Go!

A wonderful way to explore the past is through oral history. You can create your own by recording the stories either with a video camera or tape recorder. Future generations will thank you!

If it's the future you seek, watch *The Jetsons* and other futuristic TV shows for inspiration and then create the future as you envision it. Be an innovator and come up with an invention for the future. Get out a drawing pad and draw the latest fashion designs—maybe even create new modes of transportation and communication. Make up a new sport or game; develop words that correspond to your new environment. The future is yours to see, so make it fanciful and fun.

Combine all your predictions into a book or home video for future reference to see how well you did. You may want to predict the future a year, 5 years, 10, or 100 into the future. Prepare a time capsule preserving the past and your future predictions. Choose things that say something about you, such as photos in your favorite outfit or standing beside your favorite mode of transportation. Cut out top news stories of the day and hometown stories, such as who won the basketball game. Add these to the time capsule. Also make room for your book of predictions. Put everything into a box, trunk, plastic storage box, or tin. Close the box with tape and a notation that this time capsule is not to be opened until a specific date. Then bury it, hide it away in the back of a closet, or put it in the attic until it's time to open it.

Time travel into the past or forward to the future can be a real family adventure!

On the Job

For most of us, our neighbors' lives may appear to be very much like our own. Children go to school, parents work nine-to-five jobs, and they shop at the local grocery store and go to a movie theater or ballpark. We see them at church, on our daily walks around the neighborhood, or at the local pizza parlor. Regardless of how similar our daily lives and routines may appear from the outside, however, we might find them quite different as we explore their jobs and way of life as it pertains to work. The daily routine of a retail store owner is quite different from that of a restaurant server, farmer, truck driver, firefighter, or office worker. The work, the hours, the dress, and the responsibilities are all different. Looking at different lifestyles and talking with people about their careers can be a learning experience for the entire family. Exploring different lifestyles may open new possibilities to children as to what they want to do when they grow up and what they might expect on the job.

What You'll Need

◆ A list of occupations of family, friends, and neighbors

Consider spending a day with a local farmer. Regardless of the type of farming, farmers are usually up at the crack of dawn to feed the animals, milk the cows, or prepare to head out to the fields to plow or harvest. Do you really know how milk gets to your local market? Visiting a dairy farm will help you appreciate all that goes into getting milk to your supermarket and in your glass. There is much more to the job than just milking the cow and shipping out the milk. What about the fruits and vegetables you enjoyed today? A great place to learn about how they are grown is to visit with one of the farmers at the farmer's market. In order to understand the entire process, it would be beneficial to make it a seasonal adventure, visiting with farmers during all seasons to see what is required from preparation to planting to harvest time.

One way to get started on a farming lifestyle adventure is to find out whether there are any local farm tours. These often happen in the spring, just as everything is beginning to grow. There are also farms that let you pick your own strawberries, blueberries, apples, and other fruits and vegetables. In autumn, some farms celebrate the harvest season. Not only can you pick out your favorite pumpkin for Halloween, but you can also go for a hay ride and see the farm at harvest time.

Easy Does It

Ask a farmer whether your family can come visit for a day and help with the chores or at least get a one-on-one tour of a farming operation. Smaller, local farmers are more likely to accommodate you. But remember, this is their job—and they may not feel they have time for a tour. So don't be disappointed.

To help kids understand the seasonal changes that affect farm life, you may want to plant a small kitchen garden. It helps to understand the life cycle of plants and how a farmer's life revolves around planting, tending, and harvesting. Next time you are driving through the country, see how many different crops you can recognize. Keep a tally to see which family member identifies the most.

What child hasn't aspired to becoming a firefighter? Kids love visiting a fire station to see the big red trucks, the brass pole, and—in some instances—the Dalmatian that hangs out with the firefighters. Talk with a firefighter and find out what his or her schedule is. Often, they work several days in a row and then are off several days. Learn about the types of training that firefighters have to complete before actually getting on that truck. Find out what his or her chores are at the fire station. Ask the firefighters about the clothing and gear they are required to wear and/or carry. Being a firefighter can seem extremely exciting, but it's also hard and often dangerous work.

Know a truck driver? Without truck drivers, there would be nothing at the mall or supermarket. Almost everything is shipped across the United States by truck. Your neighborhood truck driver may carry the mail or whatever load is available, from fruits and vegetables to furniture, various goods for resale, or gasoline. Next time you are on a trip, count the various trucks you see on the highway. See how many different kinds of goods you can identify for each truck.

If you know someone who is a truck driver—whether a local driver or one who drives long distances—ask whether he or she would take some time to visit with your family and explain what knowledge is necessary in order to do the job. Ask about riding on a short jaunt with him or her if possible. If not, you can still learn about a truck driver's lifestyle—and maybe he or she will give you a tour of his or her home away from home. Ask that person whether he or she goes out for several days or weeks at a time driving cross country, or are the routes local or day trips to nearby towns? What does the truck carry? Have you ever really thought about how all our food gets from the farm to the market or how our clothes get from the manufacturer to the retail store? What credentials do you need to drive a big rig, and how do you get them? What are some important things you need to know to drive a big truck? Does the truck driver have to wear a uniform? Where will he or she sleep at night while on the road—and if he or she sleeps in the truck, what about a shower? Truck driving is not a nine-to-five job, but it is essential—and we all depend on truck drivers each day.

Have you ever thought about what's required to be a shopkeeper? There's a lot more to retail than

Way to Go!

After spending time with someone learning about his or her profession, be sure to send a note of thanks to show your appreciation.

selling things all day. You have to purchase the goods to be sold, inventory and stock them, and then figure out how you will market them to your customers. If you do a great job of marketing, then you will sell a lot of goods and have to account for the money you received for them. Find a local shopkeeper and ask whether you can interview him or her. Older children may like to help receiving goods and stocking shelves. You will find that a shop owner often has to wear many hats to get the job done every day.

Have a conversation about all the things one needs to know to be a shopkeeper. Let the kids play pretend store. They need to think of a store name and make posters advertising the store. They will want to stock the shelves—a grocery store with canned goods should be easy to set up from the kitchen pantry. All the goods need to be priced. Sale signs need to be made or a flyer advertising their wares. And they need money that has to be counted. You could use play money or actual pennies depending on the age level of children involved.

Did You Know?

♦ A logger has one of the most dangerous jobs.

♦ There are 152.8 million people age 16 and older working in the United States.

♦ There are approximately 253,000 firefighters in the United States.

♦ The United States has about 98,000 people who prepare taxes.

♦ There are 4.8 million people in the United States who work at home.

So ... what do Mom and Dad do all day at work? Why not plan a visit to their workplaces? Many companies participate in "Bring Your Son or Daughter to Work Day," which takes place on the fourth Thursday in April. Participating companies may have activities and handouts especially for celebrating the day.

This is a great way for children to see where Mom or Dad goes each day when heading off to work, and it can be a real treat for both parents and kids. It's a great time to introduce the children to workplace colleagues and show off the kids. Visiting the workplace will also help kids understand how the job relates to their everyday lives. Being on the job not only gives insight to children about work but also helps adults realize their significant contributions.

Once the kids are home and have time to think about your job, they may want to emulate your workplace. If you work in an office, help them set up a pretend office. Offer other guidance as to what you do. Work isn't such a mystery once they understand what you do.

Your on-the-job adventure is a great learning tool that helps the entire family appreciate the work being done. It also helps each of us understand how our lives interact and overlap as we perform our daily tasks on the job and experience yet another backyard adventure.

Lend a Hand

Many people feel a need to volunteer during the holidays, but why not help out other times of the year when volunteers are scarce and many nonprofit organizations can use a helping hand? Nonprofits depend on volunteers to help with the workload, such as administrative duties, stuffing envelopes for direct mailings, organizing fundraising events, manning food and clothing collection drives, or providing services to clients. Some nonprofits to consider are Habitat for Humanity, a local animal shelter, a literacy council, Ronald McDonald House, Big Brothers Big Sisters, parks and recreation centers, after school programs, senior citizen centers and retirement homes, and homeless shelters. These places will give you the opportunity to work in a soup kitchen, provide support at the animal shelter, teach someone to read, invite a homeless or at-risk child to share in family outings, help with building houses for the homeless, visit the elderly, or clean up parks and public recreation areas. Any way you look at it, this is a win-win activity for all involved.

What You'll Need

◆ A list of volunteer opportunities in your neighborhood

Before you get started, you will want to find out what nonprofit organizations are in your backyard. Spend time as a family learning about the various organizatons, and choose two or three that appeal to you. You may find you have an interest in helping the homeless with food through various soup kitchens or housing through organizations like Habitat for Humanity. Perhaps you are a family of animal lovers. Consider the local humane society or other animal rescue organizations. While you may not be able to work directly with the animals, you can raise money and awareness of the cause through charity events or requesting donations. The cause may hit close to home, such as cleaning up a park or building playground equipment for the neighborhood park—or far away, such as raising funds for food, healthcare, and education for children in a third-world country.

Did You Know?

◆ Forty percent of the U.S. homeless population is families with children.

◆ About 1 in 20 U.S. adults are unable to read a newspaper.

◆ There are approximately 7 million homeless pets in the United States.

◆ Approximately 61 million people volunteer through or for an organization in the United States.

◆ The American Red Cross was founded by Clara Barton and friends in Washington, D.C., in 1881.

◆ Habitat for Humanity has built more than 225,000 houses around the world.

◆ "Trick-or-Treat for UNICEF" began with a group of Philadelphia trick-or-treaters and their pastor in 1950.

Once your family members have settled on the agency or organizations that they want to help, find out what is needed and then figure out how the entire family can pitch in. Do they need volunteers to help with a fundraising event such as a golf tournament, 5K run, bake sale, or yard sale? You may want to participate in the 5K run as a family soliciting donations from friends and family. An agency may need someone to help with stuffing envelopes for their next direct mail campaign or help collect food and clothing. Animal shelters are always looking for donations of clean towels, blankets, pet beds and toys, and other supplies. It may be that because of the variety of ages and abilities in your family, there are several ways the organization can use your time and skill. All the while you are helping you are also enjoying a family adventure that not only enriches your family's life but helps others.

In addition to helping an organization, the family or individuals may want to initiate their own charitable activity. Start a loose change jar, and compete to see who can collect the most money during a specific period of time. Even the smallest donation is important and can help. The birthday boy or girl may want

Way to Go!

If you're interested in one-on-one client services, by all means take advantage of any special training that organizations offer to volunteers.

to request a small contribution for their charity in lieu of or in addition to presents. Offer to collect clothing or canned goods in your neighborhood that can be donated to various charities. Use your imagination. What talents and skills do you have to offer that will help not only the nonprofit organization but the clients they service? Whatever you contribute to charity, you will find that it is a fulfilling experience and a wonderful family adventure.

Lending a hand is a great way for a family to come together—working, learning, and experiencing a new adventure that benefits their own backyard.

Trading places can be a real backyard adventure. It's a great way to learn more about your family, your neighbors, and different cultures. You can explore how it would be to live in different time periods or work various jobs. And through volunteer activities, you can contribute to your community and have fun. Trading places can provide serious exploration of life—a fulfilling backyard adventure.

Chapter 5

Creative Spirit

In This Chapter

- ◆ Creating handmade paper
- ◆ Fun with clay: a primer on clay creations
- ◆ An artistic adventure
- ◆ Gardens … from pots to tepees
- ◆ Exploring your talents

Exploring your creative spirit can be a great adventure. There are many fun learning experiences available, from week-long stays at artist enclaves to music camps. But you don't have to go on the road to find your creative spirit. Look in your backyard for opportunities to learn a new skill or technique. High schools and community colleges often offer continuing education classes that include how-to courses such as quilting, gardening, photography, computer maintenance, and language. You can also check around for individual artists who teach craft, sewing, painting, or woodworking classes in their studios or homes. You can meet artists and ask about classes at craft fairs and art exhibits. Many arts and crafts and fabric stores also offer classes. Home improvement stores offer classes on topics from building a birdhouse to tiling your bathroom floor. Don't forget the how-to books at the library and the television channels dedicated to inspiring and showing you how to tap into your creative spirit.

There are several ways to approach this adventure. Is there a particular project that you want to complete, or is there a craft or skill that you want to cultivate? If this is going to be a family affair, decide on a project to work on together—one that will benefit the entire family. Or your family may want to each explore their very own creative spirits and choose from several different skills or projects. You may even decide to work in teams, helping each family member work and complete their own project. And if you can't make a choice, why not try a variety of how-to classes and see which one speaks to you? Whether you're interested in a day or a lifetime of creativity, a creative adventure is as close as your backyard.

See Appendix A for suggested books and websites relating to the activities in this chapter.

Paper Crafts

Ever wonder where paper comes from? It has been used for thousands of years in various sizes, shapes, and forms. Paper is so commonplace it is hard to conceive of how one makes paper. The word "paper" comes from papyrus, a type of reed plant grown in Egypt. The Egyptians, Greeks, and Romans laid strips of papyrus cross-wise, pounding it into a flat sheet of "paper."

Papermaking as we know it is more closely associated with China, where it is believed to have been invented around the second century B.C. This paper was made from a pulp of fibers: silk, cotton, and other plant materials. These fibers are pulped in a mixture that has the quality of oatmeal. It is mixed into vats of water. Using a two-piece frame called a deckle and mold, the pulp is scooped up onto the frame, shaken to distribute the pulp evenly, then cast off the frame on to a cloth for drying. The cloth-covered papers are piled together, the water pressed out, and then left to dry. That is a very concise description of how handmade paper is created. You can still see this basic technique used today in India and other parts of Asia where many decorative papers are made. Paper artists use this method as well, adapting it to their needs.

Did You Know?

- The Moors from North Africa brought papermaking to Spain and Portugal when they invaded Europe in the twelfth century.

- Rice paper is made from the mulberry tree.

- Parchment is a type of paper made from animal skin.

- In the Americas, Mayans were making paper called amati as early as the fifth century.

- Amati comes from the bark of a variety of fig trees.

The finest early papers were treated with immense respect and were used to record ancient sacred texts. As the craft developed, more inferior grades of paper were made and used to print paper money, wrapping materials, and even clothing.

For many years, we've relied on machine-made papers that come in a variety of sizes, textures, and colors but don't have the eye appeal or texture that you find in handmade paper. A great deal of beautiful decorative paper is now being imported and used in art projects, greeting cards, lampshades, book and journal covers, mattes for framing, and table decorations. Papermaking is easy—so why not find your creative spirit in a papermaking adventure?

What You'll Need

- A blender

- A plastic dishpan or sweater storage box to use as a vat

- Papermaking kit(s) and/or paper to be recycled

- A cotton linter (available at hobby shops and arts and crafts stores)

- A deckle and mold

- Fabric or interfacing sheets

- Sponge

◆ A rolling pin

◆ An old colander or strainer

◆ Bucket

One of the methods of papermaking common in Asian countries—and the method that traveled to the West—is very similar to how handmade paper is made today. It starts with finely shredded cotton or silk fibers that are blended, molded, and dried. Although modern techniques and assembly line modifications have been made, you can still watch papermakers in India practice the technique much as it has been done for centuries.

You can purchase papermaking kits in many arts and crafts stores or online. These come with the deckle and mold as well as the cotton linter and instructions. Some kits come with decorative additives. However, most everything you need you will find in your kitchen and craft supplies.

Papermaking is a great summer adventure. It's wet and messy, so it's great for doing outside. You can get started by recycling computer or copy paper, stationery, old checks, or paper produce cartons such as blueberry and tomato cartons. Papermaking doesn't take much equipment. You can pick up a blender at a yard sale or thrift shop (designate it for paper-making only). An embroidery hoop is easy to use if you don't have or are not ready to make your own deckle and mold. Purchase a plastic dishpan or sweater storage box to use as a vat. An old colander or strainer comes in handy for draining water from the pulp. Use leftover interfacing or cotton fabric for drying cloths. A rolling pin or wine bottle is great for pressing and rolling the paper into flat, thin sheets. These common household items are all that is necessary to get you started making paper.

There are several easy methods for quick papermaking. The easiest is to use fiber screen wire stretched tautly inside a plastic or wood embroidery hoop. Yes, it will be round, but it will help you get the feel of making paper without a lot of work or expense. After you try your hand at a simple method, you may want to make larger pieces using a deckle and mold.

You can even use recycled papers. The criterion for a suitable paper is that it has some long fibers in it to hold it together. Cotton linter added to recycled paper will provide the needed fibers. To identify good paper, hold it up to the light. If there is a watermark that says "cotton," you will know it has cotton fiber in the paper. Computer paper as well as most other machine produced paper has been so overly processed that it does not work well alone and results in paper that will not stick together and will become brittle when dried. Using a mixture of half cotton linter and half recycled paper will produce an acceptable paper. Do not use newspaper or slick magazine papers as the heavily inked papers will make a gooey mess.

Way to Go!

You can add texture, color, and other decorative items to your paper by adding colored tissue paper, colored construction paper, flower petals, and snippets of thread and ribbon to the pulp. As you learn the skill, you will want to experiment with other decorative touches such as embossing and layering. You will find that the more paper you make, the more you want to experiment with new ideas.

To make paper pulp, tear paper into 1" pieces and place in blender at a ratio of one part paper to three parts water. Blend on high one to two minutes until the mixture is a smooth, creamy consistency. Repeat this process until the desired amount of pulp is made. Pour the pulp into the vat, making a mixture of approximately 90 percent water to 10 percent pulp. Mix well with your hand.

To screen the paper pulp, use a piece of fiberglass screen stretched in an embroidery hoop instead of a deckle and mold. Agitate the pulp with your hand to bring the paper fibers to the surface. Dip the embroidery hoop at a 45° angle into the pulp, turning it horizontal, passing it through the water and pulp, and lifting the hoop straight up out of the water. Carefully tilt the hoop at an angle over the pan to drain as much water as possible.

The final step is couching (removing the paper from the mold for drying) and drying the paper pulp. You can leave the paper on the embroidery hoop screen to dry or carefully turn it upside down on a piece of fabric or interfacing. Sponge the back of the screen to remove water and release the paper. Starting at one side, ease the hoop away from the sheet of paper. Place another piece of fabric on top and roll with a rolling pin. Remove the top piece of fabric and place the paper and bottom piece of fabric on a smooth surface to dry. If the sheet is not satisfactory, remove the paper pulp and return it to the vat.

Strain the pulp through colander positioned over a bucket. Squeeze out as much water as possible and pour into plastic bags. The mixture will keep for one month in the refrigerator or indefinitely in the freezer. Pulp can also be tied in cheesecloth and allowed to dry for later use.

Easy Does It

After making paper, do not pour leftover pulp/water down the drain. It will clog it up. Instead, recycle it in a compost bin.

Beautiful handmade papers often have additions of colorful threads, flowers, leaves, and other bits of paper. While the easiest method of making paper is from cotton or silk fibers, paper can be made from bark and grass fibers from numerous plants including bamboo, beach grass, cattails, corn shucks and leaves, kudzu, and okra. As you become more advanced in papermaking, you may want to experiment with a variety of fibers—but for your first papermaking adventure, recycled paper and cotton linter are the easiest and quickest way to successful papermaking results.

Don't stop there. Once you have created your own paper, you will want to enjoy it and share it with others. For starters, you can craft it into holiday cards, ornaments, or jewelry. You can also use it to cover boxes and lampshades or make book covers. Make your own journal or photo album using your own handmade paper. You don't have to go beyond using recycled paper, but if you do, you'll want to learn what plant fibers are appropriate for making paper. This backyard adventure will bring joy year round.

Potter's Paradise

For centuries, potters have been making containers and decorative objects from clay. Clay can be found almost everywhere in the world, and you may even have some in your backyard. You can recognize it because it is very shiny when wet. To test it, dig up some dirt, add enough water to make it the consistency of bread dough, and then press it in your hand. It is probably clay if it holds together instead of falling apart when you stop pressing. But even if you do have clay in your backyard, you probably don't want to start by digging your own—and you don't have to. There are so many kinds that you could spend the entire summer exploring the wonderful world of clay.

Did You Know?

♦ Remains of pottery have been found in every ancient civilization.

♦ Ceramics, earthenware, stoneware, and porcelain are all referred to as pottery.

♦ Greenware is clay that has almost dried but has not been fired.

♦ Earthenware is fired at temperatures in the range of 1,000 to 1,200 degrees.

♦ Slip is a liquid clay that is poured into a plastic mold. After the outer edge dries, the remaining slip is poured off—leaving a hollow piece of ceramic ware.

Earthen clay is what we generally think of when we talk about pottery and working with clay. But today, there are numerous kinds of clays available—and you can even make your own. At one time or another, you and your kids have probably worked with homemade clay made from flour and salt. These are quick, inexpensive alternatives, but there are several varieties on the market that are reasonably priced and easy to use. For example, there is Play-Doh (especially popular with young children) and Creative Paperclay (also nontoxic; it feels similar to earthen clay and can also be air dried). Polymer clays—which are not clays at all but PVC with liquid plasticizer—have all the properties of clay. Two well-known brands of polymer clay are Fimo and Sculpy.

What You'll Need

- A table or other flat surface that can be easily washed
- Clay
- A rolling pin
- A dull kitchen knife
- Cookie cutters

Play-Doh is a great way to get little ones started creating. It comes in fun colors; it is nontoxic, and it's easy for little fingers to squish. Of course, you will start with the snakes. See who can make the longest one. Try braiding different colors together to make multi-colored snakes. Do take note that the colors will get mixed up if you roll them all together, though.

Once they get really good at making snakes, show them how to turn them into coiled containers and add coiled lids. Another fun project is a coiled bird's nest filled with tiny eggs made from many colors of clay.

Go through your kitchen utensils and pull out that extra rolling pin and cookie cutters you never use and dedicate them to creative endeavors. Using that discarded rolling pin, roll out the Play-Doh to about a half-inch thickness and then let the kids use the cookie cutters to cut out shapes that can be decorated with bits and pieces of different colored Play-Doh. Or build little boxes using the rolled out clay. Using a dull kitchen knife, cut squares out of the clay and fit it together into cute little boxes.

Make little pinched pots by rolling up a ball of clay, sticking your thumb in the center, and then pinching out the center—working your way around the pot. Using the pinching method, you can also mold clay into objects such as animals.

Creative Paperclay feels similar to earthen clay. It can be molded and shaped just like regular clay—even allowing for fine details. It does not have to be fired, though. And once it is air dried, it is very lightweight and durable and feels much like a soft wood. It can also be carved or sanded after it has hardened. Once it has dried, it can be painted just as you would wood or paper. To protect the finished work of art, it should be sealed with a coat of lacquer or varnish.

Paperclay can be used by all ages and skill levels. Therefore, when you are ready to start keeping your creations, you may want to move on to air-dried Paperclay. Use it to create ornaments, miniatures, jewelry, dolls, or heads for puppets.

Probably one of the most familiar examples of beautiful artwork using polymer clays is the millefiori beads and jewelry often showcased at arts and crafts shows. Nontoxic polymer clays contain a base of PVC and one or more kinds of liquid plasticizer to keep it soft until it is cured. It feels and handles similar to regular clay but does not require kiln firing. Curing or hardening is achieved by baking and can be done in a typical home oven at around 275 degrees for 15 minutes. Polymer clays come in a wide variety of colors and can be used to create the same type of objects you would create using regular clay as well as the wonderful millefiori beads and jewelry.

Way to Go!

Play-Doh is meant to be reused, so don't plan on drying your creations or they will crack. If someone forgets to put the lid on tightly, you may be able to revive the Play-Doh. Moisten a paper towel and place it inside the can, closing the lid tightly. Let it sit overnight.

Your best bet is to start out trying all these clays and more until you find the medium and method that best suits your needs and what you want to create.

Start with achievable goals, pinch pots, slab boxes, and coiled bowls and move on to more difficult projects. Using some of these simple methods will allow for creativity and a feeling of success without spending a lot of money or time. You'll soon be addicted and moving on to more elaborate projects, such as miniatures for dollhouses or train sets, beads, jewelry for gifts—and who knows, maybe an elegant vase for your dining room table.

If you find that you are interested in working with earthen clay, investigate classes and workshops. Many art departments and parks and recreation centers offer classes in pottery. There, you will learn to sculpt, pour slip into molds, build slab or coil-style containers, or throw a pot on a potter's wheel. And if you find that you love the pottery but not the clay, or you just don't have the time for throwing your own pots, try one of the many shops that offer paint-it-yourself greenware. For a small fee, they provide the greenware, finishing instructions, and firing. Make learning to make your own clay creations a family adventure.

Artist's Colony

Great art doesn't happen overnight. It is the result of many hours of experimentation, exploration, and ongoing creation. If you have a budding artist in your midst, you may want to plan a backyard adventure that encourages that talent—and in the process, you may find more than one artist in your family. Think about Grandma Moses, who began her art career while in her '70s. It's never too late to try your hand at creating beautiful art.

You may have already explored papermaking and pottery, but don't stop there! There are so many other artistic and creative venues to explore. You will find that learning a variety of mediums and techniques often augments your skill and opens the door to increased creativity.

What You'll Need

- Paper
- Pencils, colored pencils, crayons, and markers
- A clipboard or drawing board
- Paints
- Paper plates or the lids from deli containers for mixing paints
- Scissors
- Glue
- Rubber stamps for printing
- Ink pads (optional)

You probably already have pencils, markers, crayons, chalk, and watercolors in the house. You may have acrylics or craft paints. Purchase charcoal pencils, newsprint or sketchpads, or a pad of watercolor paper. To hold the paper and have a hard surface to work on, tape the paper to a piece of Masonite board or use a clipboard.

Start with drawing. All kids love to draw. Get out the pencils, colored pencils, crayons, markers, and lots of paper in all sizes (the bigger the better). Have them draw pictures of themselves, each other, their family and pets, and their house or school. Or, have them draw whatever they can imagine—from blue dragons to purple trees. If you have a long hallway or a stairwell, hang the masterpieces on the wall and have an exhibit.

Another day, you may want to draw from real life. Go on an excursion to the backyard or a park. Take a sketchbook or sheets of paper clipped to a clipboard. Find an inspiring view to capture. It may be one or several flowers in the garden, a magnificent old tree, or a little sister playing in the sandbox.

Way to Go!

Tape may take the paint off your walls. If you do use tape, pull the piece off and tape it to a piece of cloth before putting it on the wall. The cloth takes away some of the stickiness.

Encourage your young and old artists alike to draw what they see and feel—to step outside the box. You may get a totally different perspective from each artist. Always remember that artwork is the artist's interpretation of the scene—and that means it doesn't have to be a realistic rendition. For fun, try having everyone draw the same scene. Hang the finished drawings side by side to see how each person perceived the same subject.

If it's a cold rainy day, set up a still life in the kitchen. You could use a bowl of fruit or a vase with flowers. A still life is even better for comparing each artist's perspective of the same view. Or, have each child do several renderings of the same still life—changing the style, method of drawing, or medium used. Try contour drawing. Place the pencil on the paper and draw only one object in the still life without ever looking at the paper.

Painting also offers a world of exploration. You may choose ethereal, pastel watercolors; bold, bright acrylic paints; or thick, layered oils. Acrylics are the easiest to use. The consistency of the paint makes it easy to apply and clean up. Acrylics come in a variety of vibrant colors.

Watercolors offer the serendipity of the unexpected—especially if you paint on damp paper. Use masking tape to tape the paper to your board or clipboard, then use a sponge to dampen the paper. Immediately brush with watercolor paint and watch it run across the paper. Learning to control this scattering of color is the delicate beauty of a watercolor painting.

Did You Know?

♦ Red, yellow, and blue are primary colors. You can't make them by mixing any other colors.

♦ Grandma Moses was in her seventies when she began painting.

♦ Pablo Picasso is known as the most prolific painter per the *Guinness Book of World Records*.

♦ The oldest known paintings are in a cave at GrotteChauvet in France. They are estimated to be 32,000 years old.

♦ Georges Seurat used tiny dots of paint to create *A Sunday Afternoon on the Island of La Grande Jatte*. This pointillist creation took him two years to complete.

We generally associate oil paintings with the masters of the Renaissance. Oil paints are really not that intimidating, but they are not as easy to work with as acrylics or watercolors. And oil paints and brushes can a bit expensive.

Printing or rubber stamping has become a huge phenomenon with the scrapbook set. Stamps are also used widely for making your own cards. Stamps are easy for little ones to use to create their own artwork. But there are so many uses for stamps that older children will be enthralled once they begin exploring.

Just for fun, have a scavenger hunt around the house to see how many things you can come up with that would work for stamps. Bottle caps make great circles; pencil erasers can be used for polka dots; and leaves with heavy veins make beautiful leaf prints. Try a comb for wavy stripes. You may even want to make your own sponge stamps using the dehydrated sponges you can pick up at arts and crafts stores. These are flat sponges about ⅛ inch thick. Use a cookie cutter or a stencil to draw a design on the sponge, or draw your own freehand design. Cut it out and put it in water. Presto! You have a sponge stamp!

For beginners, use water-based acrylic paints. Pour a little on a large, flat surface (a paper plate works great). Dab a little paint on the surface, and print on a piece of paper. Fill a few pages with your great stamps, let them dry, and keep them for other art projects.

Once you get the hang of stamping, why not have a family stamping party and stamp your own gift wrap and cards? Kraft paper, white wrapping paper, or tissue paper is all good paper for gift wrap. For cards, pick up some card stock, cut it in half, and fold it over. You now have blank cards perfect for printing. Invitation envelopes are just right for your cards and can be found at most office supply stores.

Older kids can stamp book covers, create cards and invitations, and make special paper for their scrapbook pages. And Mom, why not pick up a white tablecloth and napkins to stamp in your own decorative style? There are special inks and paints that can be set with a little heat from the iron.

Once you see all the wonderful art you can create using stamps, you will want to check out ready-made stamps. Or, you may want to create your own intricate stamps or explore other printing methods such as monoprints (a form of printmaking where the images or lines cannot exactly be reproduced). The entire family will be pleased and amazed at all the wonderful things they can create with a minimum of materials and lots of imagination.

A collage is a picture made by sticking bits and pieces of paper, ribbon, cloth, photographs, and other found objects onto a surface. Remember when I said to keep all those pages of printed paper? Now you can use them and any handmade paper you have available. Look through your watercolor paintings; you may have a few that you only like parts of, so cut out that portion and use it. Incorporate some of your pressed flowers from your botany adventure (see Chapter 2) or add photos of your insect collection (see Chapter 2). Tear pieces from magazines and the newspaper; add bits of ribbon or interesting threads. There are no rules; just have fun and make something that is pleasing to your eye.

Now that you've tried a few techniques and used a variety of mediums, it's time for inspiration. Look around you at the works of art in your house—from the decorative printed paper towels to the prints and paintings on your living room walls. All these were created by an artist or a designer using some of these same techniques. Look at ads and photo layouts in magazines for ideas. Check out art books from the library; study the Renaissance masters, Picasso's cubism, Georgia O'Keefe's big, bold, beautiful flowers, or Seurat's pointillism. Also look at books of architecture, textiles, and photography. All of these will give you inspiration for your next artistic creation. Visit museums, galleries, and art fairs to see what other artists are creating.

If there's a real interest, check with your local arts center, art supply store, parks and recreation department, or community college for drawing and painting classes. Maybe you can set up an appointment with a local artist or art teacher for some private lessons. Creating tends to free the spirit, relax the mind, and present the joy of fulfillment. Doesn't that make for a great backyard adventure?

Sowing Seeds

Do you like to play in the dirt? Plant a garden. What fun it can be watching dinner grow! Be creative in planning and planting your garden. A garden can be a regular vegetable garden, an herb garden, or an annual or perennial flower garden. You may want to plant a garden that attracts birds or butterflies. Maybe you want to grow just pumpkins, several varieties of lettuces, or all white flowers. A garden doesn't have to be a rectangle with nice, straight rows. Try interspersing vegetables in your flowerbeds or plant a round garden, a container garden, a square-foot garden, or a green bean tepee.

Whatever you decide, you can use information you have gained from other backyard adventures (such as the insect safari and the botany exploration, see Chapter 2) to help in planning and growing your garden. If it is a vegetable garden, be adventurous and grow veggies that you like and a few you have never tried.

What You'll Need

- ◆ Gardening catalogs
- ◆ Seeds and/or plants
- ◆ Container(s) and/or garden space
- ◆ Potting soil

- Fertilizer

- Basic gardening tools: trowel, spade, garden hoe, and watering can

Seed catalogs come out in late December or early January. Look through catalogs for ideas and information about different varieties of plants. Find out what will grow in your weather zone. Go to your local library and check out some gardening books. You don't have to wait until spring to get started. Get the kids involved. Once you figure out what plants you are interested in, give them the catalogs and let them cut out pictures of plants that they like—and glue them on a large poster board (their own little garden). Of course, you could create your own paper garden, too. Come warm weather, you can replicate the paper gardens in your yard.

A garden gives kids an opportunity to take on some responsibility. If they don't water and weed, the pretty flowers or big orange pumpkins may not grow. Start with a few quick growers like beans or squash to help maintain interest. No one can resist checking on how much growth has taken place overnight! Just to see how fast your beans are growing, measure the height each day and record it. Both beans and squash are easy and usually result in a plentiful crop. You might even get the kids to eat their veggies if *they* are the ones who grew, picked, and helped prepare them for dinner.

In cold climes, you can get an early start by planting your seeds in pots inside and setting them out after the last frost. It's fun to watch those little green leaves poke their heads up through the dirt, looking for sun. For a vegetable garden, try planting seeds for yellow squash, radishes, green beans, English peas, watermelon, pumpkins, and corn. These are all fast, easy growers. Tomatoes and peppers can be difficult to grow from seed, so when the season is right, pick up a couple of these plants at the garden shop.

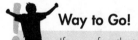 **Way to Go!**

If your family is new to gardening, start with easy-to-grow seeds or plants that are readily available from your local garden shop. Start small with one or two plants and gradually add more.

Don't think you have to plant an acre to have a garden. You may want to start very small with a few pots and do some container gardening. This is an especially simple way to introduce children to gardening. Give each child a pot filled with dirt and let them choose the seeds or plant they want to grow. Then it is up to them to make sure their garden gets plenty of tender, loving care: water, sun, fertilizer, and all those pesky weeds pulled. Another easy gardening method is a no-till method called "lasagna gardening" that layers compost and dirt instead of plowing up the grass. For something a little bigger, try a method called square-foot gardening. In square-foot gardening, you build a box with one-foot grid partitions. Within that square foot, you plant your seeds or plants. You can have one square foot or many depending on the size of the garden you want.

Did You Know?

- The most popular vegetable in America is the potato.

- Over 90 percent of all home gardeners grow tomatoes.

- The average American eats 13 pounds of tomatoes a year, and consumes another 20 pounds in the form of ketchup, salsa, soup, and barbeque sauce.

- The 10 most popular home grown vegetables in the United States and Canada are, in order: tomatoes, peppers, cucumbers, onions, beans, lettuce, carrots, sweet corn, radishes, and cabbage.

- Rosemary, sage, oregano, thyme, and marjoram all belong to the mint family.

- Bees and other pollinating insects pollinate nearly 90 percent of the world's plants.

- A Monarch butterfly will only lay its eggs on the milkweed plant, and it is the only plant the caterpillars will feed on.

While you're at it, explore companion planting—plants that grow well together. Native Americans often planted "three sisters gardens"—corn, beans, and squash. The corn provides support for the pole beans; the beans add nitrogen to the soil, which helps the corn grow; and the squash covers the ground, keeping the soil moist and minimizing weed growth. Companion planting explores this interaction between plants and takes advantage of which plants like to grow next to each other.

A butterfly garden can be beautiful and fun. Plant some of the butterflies' favorite flowers and watch them flutter around your garden. Some plants to choose from are: marigolds, red or blue salvia, purple coneflower, zinnias, alyssum, shasta daisies, and ageratum. Pick a nice sunny location either near a window or outside seating area. That way, you can be a quiet spectator enjoying both the flowers and the butterflies.

If you have the patience and want a fun little hideaway, grow a tepee garden. You will need three to five bamboo stakes at least five to six feet long. Arrange the stakes in a tepee shape, securing the top with a cord or wire, and anchor the bottom of the stakes by burying them two to three inches in the ground. For a quick, temporary tepee, plant pole beans or morning glories to wind around the bamboo stakes and train the plants up the stakes. If you want something a little more permanent, you might decide to plant honeysuckle, jasmine, or even grapes. Can you think of anything more fun than sitting in your tepee and pulling bunches of grapes off the "walls"?

Not only can the family enjoy the process of growing their own veggies and flowers, but they can also enjoy the fruits of their labor at the dinner table. Gardening is a gratifying backyard adventure for the entire family.

On Stage

Although most people say they have a fear of public speaking or being on stage, they also secretly aspire to just that—being on stage as an actor, comedian, or musician. And most families have at least one aspiring performer. But there is a lot more than just getting up on stage; lots of behind-the-scenes work has to happen. That work involves numerous people who possess a wide variety of talents and skills. An on-stage adventure is perfect for exploring those various occupations and discovering who has an interest and talent for making a great production happen.

Everyone, regardless of age, can get involved in this adventure. Younger children are often very imaginative and can come up with some fantastic twists for the story and visuals for the scenery—and because they generally love an audience, they will love to play a part on stage. Let the teens research a play or write an original play—maybe with some input from the family. As a family, you will have to decide on scenery, costumes, lighting, and props, and everyone can participate in finding the bits and pieces to finish out the setting. And of course, you will need music as a background to accent various scenes. You may have a musician or music lover in the group who wants to contribute original music or find just the right accompaniment for the scene.

What You'll Need

◆ A makeshift stage

◆ Music and props as needed

For starters, have an afternoon variety show with no special props, scenery, or lighting—just each person showing off his or her own special talents. Now that you have the stars warmed up, talk about putting on a show and inviting an audience. You may want to do something for the next family holiday, for the neighborhood block party, or for a school function. Or, maybe you just want to have fun at home as a family.

Once your family has decided on the type of performance, you need to think about whether or not you need a background or scenery, props, lighting, and music. What will you use for a stage? The living or dining room—or maybe a large porch—are all possibilities.

The variety show dressed up a bit may be a very good starting point. You've already identified each family member's talents; now all you have to do is polish the performance, set the stage, and dress for the occasion. Choose a time and a date and invite the audience. The performance can be anything—telling a joke, reading a poem, performing a magic trick, singing, dancing, doing a skit, or playing an instrument.

If you have a musical family, maybe you want to form your own family band and put on a concert. There's room for everyone to participate.

Younger children can certainly dance, sing, and play some sort of percussion instrument and have a wonderful time doing it. And it takes the pressure off the performance. No one will care whether a wrong note gets played if everyone is having a good time and enjoying performing. Who knows ... you might be the next generation family band, just like The Partridge Family!

Easy Does It

Start with something relatively easy. Don't try to put on a three-act play for your first performance!

Now that the performance bug has bitten, you may be ready to go on to something bigger. If it's a skit or a play, acting is only a small part of putting on a play or filming a movie. You will need lighting, scenery, costumes, props, and music to help tell the story. You could use a favorite children's story such as *The Three Little Pigs* or *Little Red Riding Hood*. With older children, you may want to choose a particular scene from one of their favorite books. Or, you may have a budding screenwriter in the family who wants to write an original work. If you just want to have some great family fun, why not produce your own play or home movie? Digital video and computers give you incredible editing capabilities. Instead of a week-long backyard adventure, this could be a summer project.

Did You Know?

♦ Performance art began in Greece in the sixth century B.C.E.

♦ Punch and Judy puppets can be traced to sixteenth-century Italian comedy.

♦ *Hamlet* is the longest Shakespearean play.

♦ *The Great Train Robbery* (1903) was the first narrative film, running 10 minutes long.

♦ The first video recording machine was invented in 1956 by Ampex Corporation and stood over 3 feet high and weighed over 1,400 pounds.

♦ Beethoven was the first known freelance musician because he never had a court position.

The background for your story can be a sheet decorated with markers and hung. Appliance boxes can be cut apart and painted with a landscape with clouds, trees, and flowers, or the background can be a room with drawings of bookcases, a lamp, and pictures hanging on the wall. Create a house, fort, or boat from boxes and appliance cartons. Use large pieces of cardboard for props cutting out a tree or two, a car, the sun, and ocean waves. Use your imagination and run with it. Markers and acrylic paints both work on cardboard boxes.

Think about how you will need to light your stage so that it best showcases the performance. Do you need a curtain? Who will pull the curtain, and how? Whatever props you can't or don't want to make, you will need to find elsewhere. Depending on what it is, it may just mean borrowing a couple of kitchen chairs, a stool, or other furniture. Maybe you need a sleeping bag if the story is about camping in the wilderness.

What about costumes? Depending on the story, you may just wear some of your own clothes. You may need a hat to make you look like a farmer, a cowboy, or a firefighter. Someone playing Little Red Riding Hood will, of course, need a red cape. If you have someone playing a wolf, make some ears and a tail for him or her to wear. You can also look for used props, costumes, and instruments at yard sales, thrift stores, and music stores—or try the classifieds.

Do you need music? Unless you are doing a musical, you may only need some introduction and ending music. You might need someone to help with sounds like knocking on a door, twittering like a bird, or ghostly haunting noises. If it is a musical, then by all means let the musicians use their musical talents.

Now it is time for the invitations. It all depends on who you want to see your performance. For opening night, you may just want to invite nearby relatives and friends. If it is a huge success, you can always have an encore performance.

Way to Go!

Consider videotaping performances, or give the computer whiz in the family the job of videotaping the performance, editing it, and adding commentary and music if needed. With today's technology, it's a cinch! A video of the performance proves you will really have something to show for what you did last summer. What a great gift for grandparents!

If all of this sounds like just too much to tackle, maybe your family would opt for putting on a puppet show instead of being the actors themselves. Find a few lonely socks and attach button eyes. Cut out a puppet theater from a box complete with flaps for opening and closing the stage. Presto—you are ready to put on a puppet show. Ad lib and encourage audience participation.

Once you have identified the budding actors, screenwriters, musicians, and tech people in your family, get them involved in some local productions. Look for workshops or classes in the area that interests you most—or try all of them, getting a well rounded production experience. Many areas have dance studios that teach ballet to ballroom dancing. You may also find that classes are offered at your local arts center or community college. The neighborhood church may offer choir classes. Look for music studios and shops that offer voice and instrument classes. Check the classifieds for music teachers who teach out of their studios or homes.

If you can't find a class, ask a local actor, dancer, singer, or musician about doing a one-day or weekend workshop that would introduce your family and friends to the ins and outs of performing. You may want to concentrate on one area, such as acting, or you may want to add variety and spend a couple hours experiencing it all—acting dancing, singing, and playing a musical instrument. It is all going to depend on the age group and the level of interest.

From puppet show to variety show to a full-fledged, three-act play, it can all be an exciting, rewarding backyard adventure. Join your family in exploring their creative spirit!

Chapter 6

Getting to Know You

In This Chapter

- ◆ Having an ice cream social
- ◆ Sharing fun and food
- ◆ Dinner from house to house
- ◆ Showing off your pets with style
- ◆ Having a neighborhood talent show
- ◆ Bringing the neighborhood together for food, fun, and friendship

How about sharing your backyard adventure with your neighbors? Far too often, all we do is wave to our neighbors as we leave the house in the mornings heading out to work or school or as we come in from a long day on the job. Occasionally, there may be a conversation over the back fence on the weekend when everyone is out working in the yard. But that makes for the most casual of relationships. These are people who live next door and with whom you share community. Think about how much nicer it would be if you shared fun, food, and a festival—a backyard adventure!

Although many of the activities in this book are geared toward kids, it's important that the entire family get involved. And what better way than interacting with other families in your neighborhood? This chapter is about having a family adventure. You can, of course, adapt these activities to children only. Certainly, you can have an all-kid ice cream social—but what about the adults? They still like ice cream, and what better excuse to get acquainted?

Neighborhood activities are one of the best ways to encourage camaraderie. If there hasn't been any friendly exchange beyond the waves in your neighborhood, then it's time to do something about it. And you can be the first family to break the ice by dropping by with home baked muffins or cookies and introducing your family. Once you get to know the neighbors, plan other neighborhood activities such as an ice cream social, a traveling feast, a pet parade, or amateur hour. What a great way to make new friends and build a close-knit community!

See Appendix A for suggested books and websites relating to the activities in this chapter.

Ice Cream Social

Get to know your neighbors, have a party! An ice cream social is a great, easy get-together and perfect for a summer gathering. If you are making homemade ice cream, there will be some time to wait. Because this is also a get acquainted party, plan ice breakers for the adults and fun activities to keep the kids busy while the ice cream freezes.

What You'll Need

- An ice cream freezer filled with homemade or store-bought ice cream
- Cones, ice cream dishes, and spoons
- Toppings for ice cream
- Light snacks

For a real old-fashioned party, ask everyone to bring their ice cream freezer filled with their favorite homemade ice cream mixture to freeze. Why not also have them bring their favorite recipe for homemade ice cream (a good topic for starting a conversation)? Be sure you have plenty of extra ice on hand just in case. Most everyone will probably have electric freezers, but if not, how much more fun to take turns cranking the freezer! You may even be able to get the kids to join in. You should also plan on having light snacks such as pretzels, sugar cookies, or bagel chips to nibble on—especially if you are waiting for the ice cream to freeze. Remember—the ice cream is the main course for this party!

If there just isn't enough time or space for making ice cream while you wait, ask everyone to make their ice cream at home and bring it over.

While the ice cream is freezing and the adults are getting acquainted or having a friendly discussion about the best homemade ice cream, the kids need activities to keep them busy.

Encourage the kids to have fun with some old-fashioned games such as "Simon Says," "Mother, May I?", Red Rover, Pin the Tail on the Donkey, or Ring Around the Rosie. Have colored chalk available so they can draw a hopscotch board on the sidewalk or driveway. Provide a couple long ropes for skipping rope. While all this may be just too juvenile for the 'tweens, why not put them to work recording the fun on video or digital cameras? They can take photos of each other and each family group, providing candid photos of the fun. Ask them to record names for each photo so later they can put it all together as a neighborhood photo book to be distributed to each family in attendance. What better way to preserve the good time had by all and provide your circle of friends with a neighborhood directory complete with pictures.

When the ice cream is finished, keep it cold. Set out a tub filled with ice and insert the ice cream containers in the ice. Of course, if your ice cream social group is like most, there won't be any need to worry about melting ice cream. Isn't it amazing how quickly that much ice cream can disappear?

If not everyone in your neighborhood has an ice cream maker or if you live in an apartment or condo, you can still have an ice cream social—just have everyone bring a carton of their favorite store-bought ice cream. To add to the fun, have a variety of toppings available such as chocolate chips, M&Ms, sprinkles, crushed Oreo cookies—you get the picture. You could also use a fondue pot or slow cooker to serve hot fudge or caramel sauce. Have some ice cream cones and small cups available for the younger crowd.

Inside or out, homemade or store-bought, ice cream can be messy—so think ahead. Outside on the deck, under the carport, or in the drive-way are the best places for freezing your ice cream. Do keep in mind that the salty water from the freezer will kill the grass, so make sure the runoff doesn't ruin the lawn. If the party is indoors, go for a casual around-the-kitchen table experience or use the apartment building clubhouse or social room. Cover the table with oilcloth or a plastic tablecloth; use paper plates to cradle ice cream scoops. Whatever you do, don't forget the napkins.

Did You Know?

◆ In the fourth century B.C.E., Roman emperor Nero ordered ice to be brought from the mountains and combined with fruit toppings.

◆ A milk and ice concoction was created in China around 618 C.E.

◆ Both George Washington and Thomas Jefferson served ice cream to their guests.

◆ The first ice cream parlor in America opened in New York City in 1776.

If it's an indoor party, you will want to plan some quiet activities for the kids. Get out the dominoes and set up board games and/or jigsaw puzzles. You can also set out a box of papers, stickers, crayons, and pencils so they can create some art projects. Ask them to create a picture to share with the group, and then have each child show and tell about their newly created artwork. Other quiet entertainment could be games such as hangman, tic-tac-toe, or three-in-a-row. These games only require paper and pencil and a quiet place to play.

If ice cream isn't your thing, another great summertime treat is watermelon. Who can resist cold slices of juicy watermelon? If you don't want to wait until summer to get acquainted with the neighbors, have a cookie party. Ask everyone to bring a batch of their favorite cookies and serve coffee, hot cider, hot chocolate, and milk as an accompaniment. You could also ask neighbors to bring extras for trading with other guests or just bring copies of their recipe so you can exchange recipes. Another great party for cooler weather involves soup. Ask each family to bring a slow cooker full of their favorite soup. You provide the drinks, bread, and a simple dessert.

Now you know your neighbors, and wasn't it fun? An ice cream social is a fun and easy way to get to know the people in your neighborhood.

Dinner on the Ground

Dinner on the ground is a southern tradition. It is a potluck dinner served after Sunday services on tables set up outside the church. The food is good; it is a great opportunity to visit and a wonderful excuse to overindulge. There is certainly no reason why this activity should be limited to the South or churches. Invite your neighbors to bring their favorite potluck dish and share a sunny afternoon (or snowy evening) of visiting and food.

Dinner can be held under the trees in someone's backyard, in the den with a roaring fire in the background, or at a neighborhood park, community center, or school gymnasium. If you live in an apartment building or a condo complex, use the clubhouse or room set aside for social activities. Or, if you have the room, invite everyone over to your house.

What You'll Need

◆ Neighbors, family, and friends

◆ A place to host a potluck

◆ Bread, beverages, and dessert

For a true potluck dinner, just tell the neighbors to bring something. It may be that everyone coincidentally decides to bring their version of tuna casserole. So just in case, be sure to at least have some bread, drinks, and a simple dessert (like cookies) on hand. If you don't want to take the chance of everyone bringing the same dish, assign foods by category: appetizers, salads, a casserole, meat, vegetable dishes, and desserts. You can have a pitcher of iced tea and chilled sodas, hot coffee, or cider available. Set up the food buffet style on the kitchen bar or counter or in the dining room on the sideboard.

Did You Know?

◆ Potluck originates with the combination of two English words, *pot* and *luck*. The term was used when an unexpected guest was lucky enough to find a pot of whatever food happened to be available.

◆ The *Oxford English Dictionary* traces the term "potluck" to the sixteenth century.

◆ Dinner on the ground, usually associated with Southern churches, originated when people traveled several miles to attend services. By the time church let out there was no time to go home for lunch and return for the evening meeting.

◆ Dinner on the ground is often scheduled for "fifth" Sundays—the fifth Sunday in a month.

If you know there will be small children present, enlist the help of a couple teenagers to entertain them. Even for older kids, you may be able to get a teenager to sit in and play some games with younger school-age children. That way, the little ones have some supervision, the older kids are occupied with doing a good job, and parents can talk.

Way to Go!

Make kitchen and dining room tables available for people to sit down and eat. Conversation is so much easier if you are not trying to balance your plate on your knees or worried that you are going to tip over your drink sitting on the floor. Set up card tables for the kids.

While food and conversation is the theme of the party, you may want to plan some additional activities. Ask the musicians in the bunch to bring their instruments for a jam session after dinner (even the kids will want to sing along). Set up games of checkers or chess. Have a couple decks of playing cards available for the kids to play Go Fish, Old Maid, or War.

Traveling Feast

Eating can be lots of fun at someone else's house. So pass the fun around by planning a traveling feast! Also called progressive dinners, these can be as simple or elaborate as your imagination. They can include as many people as your homes can accommodate. The dinner involves everyone traveling from house to house and enjoying a different course at each place. One family provides hors d'oeuvres; another family provides salad or soup. Travel to the next house for the entree and then on to another neighbor's home for dessert.

Did You Know?

◆ RSVP stands for "Rèpondez, s'il vous plaít," which is French for "Please respond."

◆ "Response Solicited for your Valuable Presence" is an English version of RSVP.

◆ Much of Western etiquette came from the French court of King Louis XIV.

◆ Etiquette is an old French word meaning ticket. Rules of court behavior were written on what the French referred to as "tickets".

Plan the feast around a theme such as Italian, Greek, or Mexican—or plan the menu around a holiday or seasonal theme. A theme will give you a good excuse to decorate. Make the feast even more creative by requiring that all foods be green or start with the letter B. Or just ask each participant to make their favorite appetizer, salad, entrée, or dessert. Of course, you may want to suggest that they coordinate with each other so that the foods complement each other.

This type of party works well when you live close to one another. There is no need to worry about parking or carpooling. You can walk from house to house.

What You'll Need

◆ Three or four families willing to participate

◆ An agreed-upon menu

First, you need to decide how many households you will include. There may be some people who will want to participate in the dinner but not play host this time around. Also be sure to consider home size.

Appetizers might be better suited for a smaller home, where everyone can stand while eating. For the entree, a location that has enough room for a sit-down dinner would be more appropriate. Set the number of courses, determine who will fix what, and then plan the schedule.

Assuming everyone is on your block or in your building, traveling time can be estimated at five minutes. Now, you will need to assign the courses to each family and set the itinerary. You will probably want to allow at least 30 minutes for appetizers, 35 or 40 minutes for soup or salad, and another 30 or 40 minutes for the next course (and so on). Now that we've estimated the time, you should probably go back and allow another 15 minutes at each place—especially if the group likes to talk or if a house tour is in order. This should be a leisurely dinner, so don't rush it—but more than four hours (including travel time) is too long.

You probably won't need to send out dinner invitations because everyone is probably playing both guest and host for the evening. You will want to confirm how many from each family is coming so that you can cook accordingly. Be sure to ask that everyone RSVP with a number of participants. Instead of invitations, you will need an itinerary with a timetable and the menu for the evening. This can be given out at the first house or distributed to the participants beforehand.

Each course should be prepared ahead of time and left to chill in the refrigerator or warm in the oven. Set the table prior to leaving home for the first course. This will allow for each family to serve their part of the dinner without stress.

If you are new to this concept or have a small group, you may want to organize a smaller affair with three courses and stay longer at each house. Try a three-course dinner: soup or salad, a main course, and dessert. This still makes for a nice evening and is a lot easier to organize.

If it is near the holidays, adapt the traveling feast to a cookie exchange. Each participant fixes one or two batches of cookies or another holiday treat and a couple of beverages. You will travel from house to house, enjoy cookies, admire the holiday decorations, and move on. Make enough cookies so that each participant can take home a dozen of each kind of cookie. Plan to share recipes, too.

Whatever the size or theme, a traveling feast is a wonderful opportunity to enjoy the company and camaraderie of your new friends: your neighbors. What a great backyard adventure to share!

Pet Parade

One of my fondest childhood memories is the pet parade that was sponsored by our town. We dressed our pets, trimmed our tricycles and wagons, and put on our best smiles. Everyone lined up and marched down the center of Main Street. Both kids and adults alike love to watch and be in parades. Now, you don't have to march down Main Street for this to be a great backyard adventure. It can be as simple as just your family decorating your bikes, putting a fancy collar on the dog, and parading around the block. Enlist other families in the neighborhood, and before you know it, you'll have a full-blown parade on your hands!

What You'll Need

- ◆ The family dog all dolled up

- ◆ Creatively decorated bicycles, tricycles, or wagons

Gather the neighbors together and plan a parade for your neighborhood. It can be a doggy parade only with everyone bringing their dogs dressed to the nines. There's no reason the owners shouldn't do the same! Have a contest and pick the best-dressed pet, the biggest, the smallest, the shaggiest, the best behaved, the one that most resembles his or her owner—everybody is a winner. For a small group, a straw vote is appropriate (which can be a simple as a show of hands). Take lots of pictures.

Of course, there are sure to be cat lovers in the neighborhood—and what self-respecting cat is going to allow itself to be made a spectacle? So let the cat owners and other pet owners do something else, like decorate their bikes or wagons

Easy Does It

Make sure that all dogs are on a leash. Be sure to carry paper towels and bags to clean up after them, too.

with crepe paper streamers, balloons, and signs. They could even bring a stuffed animal dressed in its finest along for the ride. Vote on the best-decorated bike, tricycle, and wagon. Choose the most creatively dressed stuffed animal.

Did You Know?

◆ There are records of religious processions and parades as early as 3000 B.C.E.

◆ Military parades were a frequent occurrence in ancient Rome.

◆ During the early Greek Olympic games, athletes paraded before their contests. This is still part of the Olympic ceremony today.

◆ In the late nineteenth and early twentieth centuries, circus parades were often an anticipated public event in small towns.

◆ Macy's Thanksgiving Day Parade was started by employees, many of whom were immigrants, in the 1920s to celebrate the type of festival they loved in Europe.

If a pet parade sounds like fun but it's not really a possibility for you because you live in an apartment building or condo complex—or you don't have a pet—have a hat parade instead. Everyone can decorate a hat to wear down the hall, up the stairs, and around the pool. Vote on the most creative, the most flowers, the tallest, the smallest ... have fun with it.

To make your parade even more fun, add music. It's a great time for teens to show off their music talents and all the hard work they have put into band practice. Have them lead the parade. No musician? Not to worry. Dig out the bells, kid's tambourine, a whistle, and a toy drum and let the little musicians have a hand at creating the music. You could even march along to great marching tunes played on a stereo.

Make the parade an annual event. Choose a special day or appropriate weekend and plan for the next big event. E-mail or post flyers to your neighbors, too, and let the neighborhood know when the next parade will be so they can either participate or be there to see it. A pet parade is a backyard adventure that creates great memories.

Amateur Hour

Everyone is a performer. The popular TV reality show "American Idol" has proven that many people want to be performers. There are sure to be a number of wannabe performers living in your neighborhood. Invite the neighborhood comic, dancer, singer, drummer, and guitar player to show their stuff in a neighborhood talent show. Not only will you get to see how talented your neighbor is, but you will also have great fun getting acquainted as you pull this backyard adventure together.

What You'll Need

- Creative performers
- A corner of the yard or living room to act as a stage
- Decorations
- Light refreshments

Someone needs to take charge and find people interested in doing a neighborhood talent show. If you don't know of anyone in the neighborhood, try contacting a music teacher or drama coach at your child's school. He or she may be interested in helping or be able to offer names of someone who would like to participate. People who enjoy performing, know other talented people, and know what needs to be done to pull the show together. Meet with these talented people, set up committees, or decide between the two or three of you when you want to do the show. Set a date (and a rain date), and get busy.

To invite the performers, it may be that the group you pulled together to create the show will be all you need. Or you may want to ask a few other neighbors or friends to participate. Decide how many performances you want to have. Too many and it could get boring; too few and it will seem like a lot of effort for a small show. The number of performances will be dictated by the age of the children performing and the length of the performance. How many can you fit into an hour, including time for introductions? You will also need to decide who will emcee the show.

First, you will need to find a stage. It may be on a deck, patio, front stoop, or just a central location in your backyard. Just how elaborate does it need to be? Do you need electricity for instruments? If so, that yard location may not work. It's better to keep things simple, without microphones or electrical equipment. The performers will have to speak or sing a little louder, and the audience will need to listen a little closer. If a dancer needs music, there is nothing wrong with using a stereo.

Now that you've identified your performers and your performance area, do you need to rehearse? A quick run-through the day before or the morning of the show should be enough. Remember, this is for fun— and the more spontaneity the better.

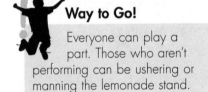

Way to Go!

Everyone can play a part. Those who aren't performing can be ushering or manning the lemonade stand.

Make flyers or invitations to send out to neighbors, friends, and family. The flyers or invitations can be as simple as letting them know a time and a place; let them know what to expect by writing a one- or two-sentence description about each participant or performance. Use your computer to print the flyers, or attach it to an e-mail message and send it.

On performance day, you will want to set up or mark off the stage area. Make it festive with balloons and paper streamers. Appoint a greeter who can also be an usher if someone needs help finding a place to sit. You may want to suggest on the invitations that they bring their own chair(s) or blanket(s) to sit on, then all you have to do is let them know where to sit.

For concessions, have some of the kids manning a lemonade stand. Ask the great cook in the neighborhood to provide cookies or other treats. You may want to charge for the lemonade and cookies and suggest a donation for the performance, giving the funds to charity afterward. The event provides a great showcase for neighborhood talent and a good excuse to visit with your neighbors as well as an enjoyable and inexpensive night out.

Instead of a talent show, your group may want to present a play or reenactment of a favorite book or historical event. This will require considerable more time and rehearsing, but it's a great way to draw on neighborhood talent and provide safe, inexpensive entertainment. And who knows—you may end up creating your own neighborhood theater company.

Did You Know?

♦ Ancient Greek plays defined theater: an audience in a half circle watching an elevated stage where actors use props to tell stories.

♦ Musical theater combines music, songs, dance, and dialog.

♦ Comedy comes from the Greek word komos, which means celebration.

♦ Plays are usually produced by a production team that includes designers for set, lighting, costume, and sound.

Do you live in an apartment building or condo complex? If it's a small production, you may be able to accommodate the audience in a corner of your living or dining room. Push the furniture against the wall and make space for your stage and audience. Then, be creative with your amateur hour. If you need more space, try the clubhouse or social activity room. If neither of these are available, then look around for another venue. A church, school, or community center might be willing to let you use their space for your show. You can offer to give a part or all of the donations you receive to their cause. And within these groups, you may also find new friends who will be interested in attending your performance or perhaps participating.

Backyard adventures are a wonderful time to get to know your neighbors. Planning activities that include residents in your neighborhood is a good way to build community spirit and pride and many wonderful memories of backyard adventures.

Block Party

Most people will agree that there are real advantages to knowing your neighbors—and even more so when you enjoy shared experiences. It's especially nice if you live far away from family. Knowing your neighbors can also make for a safer community because you will be more apt to notice a stranger on the street. Children need to know where they can turn in an emergency if Mom or Dad is unable to help. All of the activities in this chapter are ways to bring neighbors together and encourage friendship, camaraderie, and family. A block party is the culmination—a community coming together to celebrate fun, food, and friendship.

What You'll Need

♦ A committee of neighbors to plan and execute

♦ Designated space

♦ Games and activities for young and old

♦ Food and music

The first thing to decide in planning a block party is who is going to be invited. Are you going to limit it to your neighborhood, only members of the homeowner's association, your subdivision? Do you want to invite family and friends outside of the neighborhood? This will determine the extent of the planning needed. A real block party requires organization and in many instances permission from your town or city offices for such things as blocking off the street. You may also want to inquire about insurance and other legal requirements.

Did You Know?

♦ A block party is a large neighborhood celebration either to observe an event or simply for mutual enjoyment.

♦ Block parties gained popularity during the 1970s.

♦ Block parties are most commonly held on holidays such as Independence Day and Labor Day.

Decide on a date and possibly a rain date. What about entertainment and food? Are there any artists or crafts people who will want to set up a table of their wares? Do you want to set up activity tables such as face painting or hat making for the kids? Just how big or small is this event going to be? My suggestion is to start small. The first year, limit it to a few neighbors, and family. That means the logistics will be much easier and you won't have so much work to do that you can't enjoy the fun or the visiting. At a minimum, you need to get started three months before you plan to have the party. For a large block party, you will need a committee consisting of several households to hold an organizational meeting. You will want to select one member to be the main contact person—the one who is responsible for answering questions, and sending out invitations. Ask someone to contact town or city officials to determine whether any permits are needed or whether insurance is required. Appoint an activity coordinator and someone to be in charge of setup and cleanup logistics. Decide how food and beverages will be handled.

If this is the first time for a block party in your neighborhood and you are starting small, you will probably not need some of the things I've just mentioned. But even for a small event you will want to enlist some help so you can take part in the fun, too!

Approximately one month before your party, you should send out invitations. This can be done through a neighborhood newsletter, emailing neighbors, or as a flyer delivered by the kids around the neighborhood. If city permits are required, apply now. You will also want to purchase any necessary insurance to cover the event. Check on noise ordinances. If there is going to be music and it's going to be late, by all means let the neighbors know—especially those who may not be participating. You may want to have a street barricaded. If so, make arrangements with your town or city police department to do so. Make arrangements for portable toilets; otherwise, your bathroom could become the public toilet. If you need additional tables, a tent, or a sound system, then reserve that equipment at least one month prior to your party. If you need chairs, note on the invitation that guests should bring their own.

About one week before the party, confirm the placement of barricades, entertainment, food, refreshments, tents, tables, and any other necessary equipment.

Easy Does It

Do not block off thoroughfare streets without permission from city government. Also check to be sure you don't block fire hydrants.

The day of the party, make the street festive with banners, streamers, and balloons. Twinkle lights and tiki torches are festive after the sun goes down. If you weren't able to get the neighborhood garage band to provide the music, then set up a stereo system or use your computer and create a playlist of music especially selected for the event.

As you can see, a major block party can become time consuming and expensive—so as I've suggested, start small. All you really need is a little music and lots of food to get a block party started. Big or small, you will want to plan some fun activities for the kids. You can combine a block party with your talent show or pet parade. Have a jump rope or dance contest, a relay or three-legged race, set up horseshoes, croquet, badminton, and volleyball. The list could go on and on.

Getting acquainted with the neighbors at an ice cream social is only the beginning of community spirit. Continue the friendship with a potluck dinner on the ground and a traveling feast. Have fun entertaining each other. And celebrate community with a block party. Make your next backyard adventure a community coming together to celebrate fun, food, and friendship.

Chapter 7

My Town

In This Chapter

- Exploring your neighborhood
- Celebrating the uniqueness of your town
- Learning the history of your town
- Government, growth, and change

Does your neighborhood have a name? Where does your neighborhood begin and end? Do you know the names of the streets? When was your neighborhood developed? Are there any old-timers still living close by? Before all these buildings were here, what was this area? Was it an old plantation, a pasture, or an older neighborhood that was razed and revitalized or totally rebuilt? Who decides how your neighborhood changes? Does your town have a long-term plan for what will happen to your neighborhood? This chapter is about understanding your unique area, whether it's the suburbs or an inner-city neighborhood. Even in the newest housing development or the oldest neighborhood, you can find something special about the streets, buildings, and people who populate your town. No matter how old or new your town is, there is history to discover and a future to consider. Open your eyes, listen closely, and enjoy the adventure of visiting your town!

See Appendix A for suggested books and websites relating to the activities in this chapter.

Walkabout

Walkabout is an Australian term referring to a rite of passage for 13-year-old Aborigines. The six-month walkabout traces the path of ceremonial ancestors. Thus youths are learning about their heritage, community, and environs.

Now, no one is suggesting that you or your children should go on a six-month walk around your neighborhood or town—but you should at least know whether your neighborhood has a name, what the boundaries are, and what streets are located within those boundaries. It will give you a sense of place as well as familiarize you and the kids with the streets. You will not be as likely to get lost if by chance you have to detour through the neighborhood. And you will certainly be able to give better directions if you actually know the street names. It's also helpful to familiarize yourself with specific landmarks, although those can be tricky if something happens to one of them.

What You'll Need

 ◆ Walking shoes

 ◆ A notebook or sketch pad and pencil

Do you know where the city limits begin and end or which streets define your neighborhood? Go for a walk, ride your bikes, or drive around and discover the boundaries that encompass your neighborhood. Take along a notebook and a pencil. Note the streets that make up your block. What houses and other buildings are located there? How many? You can write down house or building numbers and names if they are on the mailboxes. When you get back, create a large map of the area you covered. Draw streets and add names. Draw houses and buildings, adding numbers and names as appropriate—and especially if they are neighborhood friends. You may want to color friends' houses a special color or add a star. Be sure to include alleys. You may even want to note stoplights, signs, and where fire hydrants are located.

Way to Go!

To really discover your town, one afternoon is probably not going to be enough. Reinstate the Sunday afternoon drive. Set aside some time to discover your town. Whether every Sunday for a month or several Sunday afternoons over the summer, plan what works best for your family. Each Sunday, you will want to explore a little beyond the confines of your street—expanding it at least to the boundaries of your neighborhood or to the city limits of your town.

The farther you explore, the more elaborate your map will become. Be sure to add the location of the nearest police and fire departments. Note where the library is located or where the bookmobile makes its stops. Also be sure to include walking and bike paths, parks, and play-grounds. This process will help younger children gain a sense of where they live in the big scheme of things. For older children, you may want to buy a city or county map if one is available and let them see how closely they have charted their map of the neighborhood or town.

This assumes that you live in a town. Instead of mapping out the blocks, you may find yourself mapping out the fields and country roads that make up your area of the county—all the more reason for getting acquainted with the area. In this case, you will probably want to include streams and other natural features on your map that give you a better sense of place.

If you've had fun doing this, plan other kinds of maps relating to your neighborhood. You could do a garden tour map and note where the best flower gardens or vegetable gardens are located. That way, you can make the rounds every so often to see how the flowers have changed or how the garden has grown. Kids love the wonder of things growing. Maybe there's a pumpkin patch or a row of sunflowers growing in your neighborhood. Add it to your map, and make a point of walking or rid-ing by every so often to see the new growth.

Did You Know?

◆ An aerial map is a picture of what your neighborhood looks like from the air.

◆ Cartographers are people who draw maps.

◆ The top of the map is always North.

◆ A legend is used to identify the symbols that are drawn on the map.

Another great map is one that shows the community at large. Either use the map you have drawn of your neighborhood or town or use one that may be available. Note on the map where Mom's and Dad's workplaces are located. Also note the grocery stores, schools, churches, banks, restaurants, and other significant establishments that you frequent. Now, when the babysitter is trying to explain that you have gone out to dinner, she can show the child on the map where Mommy and Daddy are and it won't seem so very far away. This kind of map will also help children relate to where their school is in relationship to home (another comforting factor if you have a little one who is somewhat afraid of being so far away from home).

To give little ones a better sense of maps, let them create a map of their most immediate neighborhood: the house. Help them draw a floor plan that shows the hallways and all the connecting rooms. Let them draw in things that make the rooms special: their bed and the kitchen table, for example. Help them with the names and explain how it is a map of the house.

A neighborhood is a place where people live, work, and play—and that includes your house. Discovering your neighborhood can be a great adventure.

Celebrate Your Town

Celebrate and appreciate the wonder and uniqueness of your neighborhood. Pretend you're an out-of-town visitor who is taking a look at your town for the first time. Get out the map you've just completed—or, if available, contact the local tourism board and ask for a map and visitor's guide. Stop by a visitor's center and pick up brochures on various attractions within the confines of your neighborhood or town. Find out whether there are any historical preservation areas or buildings in your area. Is there a wildlife preserve, a bird sanctuary, or other natural wonders?

Armed with the map and information, get out and discover the wonder and uniqueness of your town.

What You'll Need

+ Your neighborhood or city map

+ Walking shoes

+ A notebook and pencil

+ Cardstock, small boxes, and modeling clay (optional)

+ A digital camera (optional)

Our busy lives often prevent us from noticing the special qualities and uniqueness of our town. We pass the buildings and drive over the river, never thinking about how special they are. The house on the corner may have started as a one-room cabin. The library may have been donated by philanthropist Andrew Carnegie. In older areas, you can find interesting buildings with dated cornerstones, distinctive façades, and gargoyles. Many towns have historical markers that tell something about the area or the building. Look in the street for unusual manhole covers or note the interesting fence around the park or cemetery. Here, you can explore different types of architecture and designs. Look for an old train station, post office, or courthouse.

Armed with your map and tourist information, take a long, careful look at these special edifices. Notice the architecture. Does it fit in with the other buildings in the area? What is the style? What is unusual about this building? Are there gardens, fences, or walls associated with it? Play a game of pretend and imagine what it must have been like to live in that era as children and adults. How would you have dressed? Would you have been riding in a car or in a horse and buggy?

See how many building cornerstones you can find. Write down the names and dates. See who can find the most cornerstones and the oldest dates. Both the names and dates give you more information about when the buildings were built and who constructed them. Or, have the kids draw pictures of the building. They can add people and modes of transportation to their artwork.

Way to Go!

Document buildings by taking photos and labeling them to be used later when doing more research. Use the photos to put together a book about your town, showing the buildings with additional information you are able to glean from long-time residents, the library, and other historical resources.

If it's a public building or one on the historical list that is open, definitely venture in and look at the distinct style. You will also want to notice what kinds of businesses it houses or living space it provided then and now. That old, red brick building on the corner is more than just a building. Its story adds to the uniqueness of your neighborhood and your town.

In a very real sense, buildings define and hold the cultural history of towns. This may be expressed in building materials such as brick, stone, marble, steel, and glass that has been used during the town's existence. In some areas of the country, there are wonderful old houses built from rocks—often the most abundant and accessible building material in an area. The buildings that make up a town hint of its personality and style and make it distinct from all other towns. Research the stories behind the buildings—why that type of architecture was used, where the building materials came from, and how the building was used originally.

You will also want to look at how the landscape was designed around the buildings—enhancing the building as well as adding character to the surrounding neighborhood, implying community values, and sometimes dictating the use. Have each child choose his or her favorite building and draw or paint a picture, noting the important characteristics that make that building special. Also have the child choose his or her favorite part of that particular building. Older children can use cardstock, small boxes, or modeling clay to create replicas of the buildings. This is a great way to add local color to your train set or Christmas village.

Another new phenomenon in older towns is the use of murals on the sides of old buildings. While some are illegal graffiti, many murals are commissioned by the building or town as a way to promote and support the arts. Look around your town for some of these huge art projects. One of my favorite is a No. 2 yellow pencil painted on a wall at just about knee height. The pencil is about half a block long.

Easy Does It

Be sure to respect the privacy of others and don't trespass on private property.

While you are out in the neighborhood looking at buildings, don't forget to note little neighborhood parks. You may discover some real gems that you will want to come back to and enjoy another day. And while you are checking out the parks, nature trails, bike paths, and greenways, find out why they exist and whether any of them are bird sanctuaries or a wildlife preserve. Many newer developments are built around natural habitats. These are great places for walking, biking, family outings, and observing wildlife.

If you live in a new housing development, what was in the area before the development was built? If you live in the South, it may have been part of a large plantation. In the Midwest or West, the area may have supported cattle for a farm or ranch. As the buildings are constructed, can you tell what style of house will be built? Do you think the developer has a particular style of community in mind? Many new developments are being built as walkable communities with various kinds of housing, small shopping areas, and gathering areas. Explore the various types of buildings and map out the parks, bike trails, and walking paths for future use. You might even try envisioning what the community will look like in 10, 50, or 100 years from now. Does the plan work now, and will it still be viable in the future? What's missing? Have the kids imagine how it may change, and draw pictures showing those changes.

Using words, paint a picture of your town. Describe the quality of the dappled light under the old oak tree down by the lake. Talk about the white picket fence surrounding the cute little yellow house down the street. Include a description of the sights and smells of the yellow honeysuckle that covers the eave of the front porch of the house next door. Write about the tall white steeple of the old church near the center of town. Look around at all the wonder that is your town, and bring it to life.

Did You Know?

♦ Many towns have historical markers that tell something about the building, house, or particular plot of land.

♦ Historical markers are put up by national, state, or local governments. Sometimes clubs, businesses, or individuals also put up markers.

♦ Historical markers can be made of wood, metal, or stone. Some buildings have metal plaques.

♦ Those who put up historical markers strive for strict accuracy of the information. But you may want to verify the information from other sources, as well.

You have explored your neighborhood and your town—now design your own. Get out all those house plan and home decorating magazines. Let the kids cut out pictures of the houses, buildings, and landscaping to use to design a street or community that is all their own. Or let them draw up a street map and designate areas for schools, business, and housing. Tape several large sheets of newsprint together and use it to draw a city map. Draw or glue on cutouts to depict the various elements of your town. Get out little cars and people and visit your town!

Have a wonderful adventure discovering the beautiful old and new buildings that make up your town. The next time you have visitors, you will be able to show them your book of buildings and give them the grand tour without even leaving home!

Founder's Day

If your town celebrates its history or its founding fathers, you already have some sense of the history associated with your town. But maybe those who kept the founding history of your town are no longer around to pass on its story. No matter how small or how large your town or neighborhood is, there are going to be stories associated with it. Granted, newer neighborhoods may not have that many stories to tell—at least not yet. But even if the stories are of recent times, they are still worth discovering and recording for future generations.

Some places to go to gather historical information about your neighborhood are the library, school, churches, museums, historical buildings, tourism bureau, and chamber of commerce. City and county governments house many old documents and maps that will provide historical information. If there is a local newspaper, you may be able to spend some time in its archives reading old news stories. Visit old cemeteries in the area for names and dates of long-ago residents. And of course, don't forget to visit with the elderly couple who have lived on the corner for the last 50 years. Or you might find an antique dealer who is familiar with your town and can tell you about some of its previous residents. With only a little prodding, you are sure to find some great stories about your town.

What You'll Need

- ◆ A notebook and pencil
- ◆ A tape recorder
- ◆ A video camera (optional)

What's the story behind the founding of your town? The name alone may be a story in and of itself. The name may also give you some clues as to its early beginnings. Walnut Grove, Minnesota, obviously refers to the walnut trees in the area. Silverton, Colorado, derived its name from the silver mines nearby. Many towns are named for founders or settlers; for example, Raleigh, North Carolina, is named after Sir Walter Raleigh, who was the sponsor of the Colony of Roanoke. And some towns get their names from those who came before. Tuscaloosa, Alabama, is named in honor of the legendary Chief Tuskaloosa of the Choctaw Native American tribe. What's the story behind the name of your town?

Why did the settlers decide to stay at this particular place? It's obvious why a town would be built along the coast or a major waterway, due to the commerce and ease of transportation. And later, towns were built along the railroad for the same reason. Towns sprang up around gold and silver mines. Maybe there just doesn't seem to be anything quite that exciting about your town, however. Are you sure? Is it midway between major commerce centers? It may have originally been a good midpoint to stop during a long journey. Or maybe some settlers broke down in the middle of their trip west and just decided to stay. Speculate on why your town was built were it is. Then, go to the museum, library, or tourism bureau to get the real story.

Did You Know?

♦ Many small towns have some very colorful names such as Poker Flat, California; Double Trouble, New Jersey; Last Chance, Colorado; Toast, North Carolina; and Snowflake, Arizona.

♦ Some town names come from Native American words. These include such places as Manhattan ("isolated thing in water"), Chattanooga ("eagle's nest"), Topeka ("potato country"), Omaha ("upstream"), and Tallahassee ("old town").

♦ Towns with Spanish names include Santa Fe ("holy faith"), Cañon City ("canyon"), Boca Raton ("mouth of the mouse"), El Paso ("passage"), and Los Gatos ("cats").

Here in the United States, it's unlikely that your town was built on the site of a more ancient city—but it might be built on the site of a Native American campground or where the buffalo roamed. If you want to explore back even further, you may discover that a few million years ago it was a sea or a tropical paradise where dinosaurs wandered. Check out some books, go to the museum, and look at geological maps to find out what was here long before it was settled. Have the kids draw pictures of what the area may have looked liked before the town was built.

Or start with more recent history. You might want to start with newspaper archives to see what stories were in the newspaper 5 to 10 years ago. Pick up some history books and see whether there is any information of interest about the area. What explorers may have traveled through the area? While it's exciting to find out about a famous explorer who passed through your town, it can be just as much fun to find out where Grandpa kissed Grandma for the first time. They may also be able to tell you about the general store that used to be on the corner where the modern supermarket now sits and describe the people who owned it. And if your family doesn't have a long tenure in your town, then find out from others who have lived there for several generations.

Way to Go!

Your family may have a long history in your town. Ask your grandparents what your town was like when they were growing up there. They may even know some great stories that were told to them by their grandparents. Ask whether they will let you record the stories for an oral history of your town and your family's ties to the town. You can easily record them telling the stories with a tape recorder or video camera. An oral or video history is a great way to pass along your town's history to future generations.

Walking through an old cemetery will give you the names of people who lived in the area long ago. Write down the names and dates on the stones. What is the oldest date? What is the most unusual name? What is the most common name (first and last)? Note the epitaphs and write down the most interesting ones.

Armed with names, find out whether these people played a prominent role in the founding and growth of your town. Ask some of the older locals what they know about some of these people. You can also go to the library or city hall and find records and newspaper stories that may mention these names. Did any of these people play a prominent role in city or county government?

Find out whether your town has a local genealogical group. You can search online genealogical sites to see whether you can gather more information as to who these people were and what they did. Genealogy has become a major pastime, and there are a lot of people who have written books and collected stories about their ancestors and the areas they settled. These are people who would love to tell you stories about your ancestors and your town. Ask whether they will show you how to research your history or the history of your town. Ask whether you can record the stories for an oral history. If you can get printed copies, start a scrapbook of stories about your town.

Old houses have stories to tell—especially ones that may lay claim to being haunted. Why is it said to be haunted? Who has lived there, or what happened to make it haunted? It's a mystery for you to unravel. Take a notebook and tape recorder and go around the neighborhood to see what clues you can piece together from stories about the house.

Easy Does It

Don't believe or repeat everything you hear. Be a good investigative reporter and check your facts from several sources.

Where I grew up (in Cañon City, Colorado), there was an old hunting lodge on the edge of town. The story is that Teddy Roosevelt was a known visitor who came to hunt antelope before there was much of a settlement in the area. Find out what interesting secrets the old house down the street is keeping. If you can't find any, use your imagination and write a story about the house and the people who might have lived there.

In newer neighborhoods, you may have to settle for what was there before the development was built. You can begin collecting stories about your new neighborhood now to pass along to future generations. Who developed it and why? Who was the first person to move into the neighborhood? Is there anything significant about the name?

Now that you know the story behind your town, have fun sharing your adventure with friends, family, neighbors, and classmates.

Back to the Future

Your town is a very special place, but it didn't just happen overnight. It required the hard work of a lot of people over many years. Some of those people serve in city and county government offices. People have to come together to make laws and enforce them so that your town is safe. Laws, ordinances, and regulations also help decide how and where buildings will be built, where street lights and stop signs should be placed, and when garbage will be picked up. All are important issues that need to be considered in order for your town to be the very best place to live. Now, there are magazine articles about the best places in the country to live. They talk about safety, traffic, lifestyle, ease of living, and employment as well as the beautiful blue sky and the crystal clear lakes. How does your city and county government make your town the very best it can be for you now and for your future?

You also play an important role in making your town its very best. Respecting its laws, keeping the streets and sidewalk free of trash, voting, and taking an interest in the governing and planning of your town assures that your town will only get better. There's no better time than now to learn about your town's needs and to start planning for its future.

What You'll Need

♦ Dates and times of city and county council meetings

♦ A notebook and pencil

To get started, one of the first things you need to find out is where the seat of government is and who is representing you. That involves a field trip to city hall or the county commissioners' office. While you are on your mission, check out the city or county courthouse to find what important offices are located there. What services are offered by your city and/or county? In some municipalities, the city provides all the utilities for the community. In other places, the utilities do not directly fall under city/county government. Most towns have police and fire departments; however, the fire department may be a volunteer one. Most towns, even fairly small ones, have a city water system that at least provides clean, safe drinking water. Many towns nowadays offer garbage removal (not so of the very recent past). There was a time when people burned or buried their own garbage or threw it in a pit behind their houses. If there isn't already a

Way to Go!

A great activity for very young children is to learn their phone number, full name, and street address. They should also learn about 911. Visiting the police or fire departments will help them to understand the importance of being able to call 911 and who they will be talking with if they should ever have to call the number.

directory of city/county departments and offices available, then make a list of the various departments and offices and what they do. Add phone numbers, locations, and department heads (if you can find out that information). Be sure to include the county commissioner or city council member who represents your district. This is a very helpful tool you can keep for your family as well as share with your neighbors and any newcomers.

There are several different types of city government, including the mayor-council, council-manager, and city commission. Find out what kind of city government you have in your town. Find out when your town government meets and go to a meeting. Most meetings are open to the public. In many towns, the meeting is broadcast on one of the local or public television channels. It's well worth watching and a good way to find out what is going on in your town such as new retail growth, zoning changes, and decisions to pave roads, put up street signs or lights and lots of other things that have to do with running a small town. And remember that these decisions cost money. The money comes from the taxes we pay—even more reason to find out what is going on in your city government. Other units of city government such as the economic development committee or the planning department will report on their efforts to bring new business to town and how they plan to provide for the growth of housing and traffic. The chamber of commerce or the tourism bureau may report on their efforts to encourage people to move to or visit the area.

Easy Does It

Don't just show up at a city office and expect to be shown around. Call and ask whether you can schedule a time to visit and ask questions.

Observe how the group is set up and how it functions. See whether you can get a copy of the agenda from city hall beforehand. Now that you've seen the meeting, you can have a family meeting and discuss the same issues to see whether you come up with a different solution or decision.

One very important department in your town government is the planning department. City planners work with neighborhood groups, the mayor, the police, engineers, businesspeople, and many others in the community to make it the very best place to live. Remember all the buildings in your town? As the population grows, there will be a need for more housing. What if the buildings were just built anywhere. What would happen? City planners make sure towns are built so that everything fits into a nice overall plan that includes the new buildings as well as roads for traffic and a place for parks and playgrounds. Many towns have a 20-year plan. What would your 20-year plan be for your town?

Get out large sheets of paper, and using the map you created from your walkabout earlier in the chapter, draw a new grid of streets. Now, what plans would you make to ensure that your town grows to be even more special then it is today? Pretend to be a city planner who has to come up with a 20-year plan to make your town the very best ever.

The chamber of commerce and tourism bureau can be considered the marketing branch of your town's government. They let people know what is wonderful about your town. They are available to answer questions and give directions to visitors who are thinking about moving to your town as well as to tourists who just come for a short visit. How would you market your town?

Did You Know?

♦ The city planning department makes decisions about land use, including such things as where housing, stores, parks, and factories will be built.

♦ City planners must talk to people who live in the community as well as look at the impact the building will have.

♦ The mayor and city council are usually elected to office. The mayor appoints other department managers. Sometimes he or she needs the approval of the city council to do so.

♦ Towns usually have a police department that works with the county's sheriff department in protecting its residents in both the city and county.

♦ The first city police department was founded in New York City in 1844.

Think about your marketing plan for your town. Now that you have walked about and really looked at your town, what is an outstanding feature that everyone should come to see? With your building book and history research, you are well equipped to give tourists an interesting, accurate account of the founding and the history of your town. You will be able to point out the great old buildings and tell how they were used. You will have recorded stories that older locals have told that you can now pass along to the new neighbors or to your out-of-town company. What do you think is the number one reason why someone should come visit your town?

Isn't it amazing to discover adventures in your very own backyard—your neighborhood? Exploring where you live, discovering the distinctiveness of your town, and learning the history of your town is only the beginning. The adventure continues as you help shape the future of your town through participation in your local government.

Stop to smell the roses and enjoy all the wonderful backyard adventures in the place where you live!

Appendix A

Resources

Here you'll find just a short list of the resources available to you. Not only are these websites and books great for helping create the adventures in the book, they will inspire you to create your family's very own unique adventures.

Chapter 1: The Adventure Begins

Do Your Homework

Family Fun magazine and www.FamilyFun.com   Both the magazine and the website are great resources for backyard adventures.

www.homeandfamilynetwork.com/crafts/scrap.html   Offers creative ideas for a variety of scrapbooks.

www.michaels.com/art/online/static?page=scrapbooking   Provides tips and techniques for creating great scrapbooks and photo albums.

Bond, Ralph. *Family Computer Fun: Digital Ideas Using Your Photos, Movies, and Music.* Que, 2005.

McGraw, Mary Jo et. al. *Creative Cardmaking: A Complete Guide.* North Light Books, 2006.

Owen, Cheryl. *Greeting Cards Using Digital Photos: 18 Step-By-Step Projects for Uniquely Personal Greeting Cards.* Martingale and Company, 2006.

Pilger, Mary Anne. *Multicultural Projects Index: Things to Make and Do to Celebrate Festivals, Cultures, and Holidays Around the World, Fourth Edition.* Libraries Unlimited, 2005.

Scrapbooking Made Easy. Leisure Arts, 2006.

Sheehan, Kathryn and Mary Waidner. *Earth Child 2000.* Council Oak Books, 1997.

Tourtillott, Suzanne. *The New Photo Crafts.* Lark Books, 2001.

Chapter 2: Your Corner of the World

Insect Safari

www.ivyhall.district96.k12.il.us/4th/KKhp/1insects/bugmenu. html   Provides a list of amazing insects as well as photographs and facts that may be useful for science projects.

www.si.edu/resource/faq/nmnh/buginfo/start.htm   BugInfo—An entomology encyclopedia provided by the Smithsonian Institute.

http://teacher.scholastic.com/activities/bugs/   Going Bug-gy!—Offers facts and fun activities relating to insects; provided by Scholastic, Inc.

http://members.aol.com/YESedu/kidsfun.html   Kids, Bugs, and Fun!—Offers a list of insect-related activities for children of all ages.

www.ca.uky.edu/entomology/dept/youth.asp   Information about entomology for children and teachers; provided by the University of Kentucky Department of Entomology.

www.TheButterflySite.com   The Butterfly Site; contains information about all kinds of butterflies and other butterfly-related resources on the Internet.

www.earthlife.net/insects/six.html   Offers trivia and fun facts about insects.

Mitchell, Robert T., Herbert S. Zim, and Andre Durenceau. *Butterflies and Moths.* St. Martin's Press, 2001.

Zim, Herbert S., and Clarence Cottam. *Insects: Revised and Updated.* St. Martin's Press, 2001.

Backyard Botany

www.kathimitchell.com/plants.html   Plants for Kids; provides a list of links with information about various types of plants.

www.hhmi.org/coolscience   Cool Science for Curious Kids; invites children of all ages to explore botany online and in their own backyards.

www.gardenersnet.com/vegetable/dandeli.htm   The Gardener's Network; provides information about how to grow dandelions.

Brockman, Frank, and Rebecca Merrilees. *Trees of North America, A Guide to Field Identification, Revised and Updated.* St. Martin's Press, 2001.

Martin, Alexander C., and Jean Zallinger. *Weeds.* St. Martin's Press, 2001.

Zim, Herbert S. et. al. *Wild Flowers: Revised and Updated.* St. Martin's Press, 2001.

Backyard Hideaway

www.livingtreeonline.com   Provides online photos of professionally built treehouses.

www.thetreehouseguide.com   Offers information about how to build your own treehouse, plans and designs, and treehouses around the world.

Nelson, Peter, and Gerry Hadden. *Home Tree Home: Principles of Construction & Other Tree Tales.* Penguin Books, 1997.

Nelson, Peter, and Judy Nelson. *The Treehouse Book.* Universe Publishing, 2000.

Pearson, David. *Treehouses: The House That Jack Built*. Chelsea Green, 2001.

Rutter, Michael. *Camping Made Easy*. Globe Pequot, 2001.

Stiles, David, and Jeanie Stiles. *Treehouses and Playhouses You Can Actually Build*. Gibbs Smith, 2006.

Stargazing

http://antwrp.gsfc.nasa.gov/apod/astropix.html   Astronomy Picture of the Day; each day, a different image or photograph of our universe is featured along with a brief explanation written by a professional astronomer.

http://stardate.org/nightsky/   Offers weekly stargazing tips and a monthly stargazing almanac to help you plan your backyard stargazing.

http://hubblesite.org/gallery/   The HubbleSite gallery; encourages the exploration of various cosmic phenomena.

Calia, Charles Laird. *The Star Gazing Year: An Astronomer's Journey Through the Seasons*. Tarcher, 2005.

Chartrand, Mark. *Night Sky: A Guide to Field Identification*. St. Martin's Press, 2001.

Frantz, Jennifer. *Looking at the Sky*. Grosset & Dunlap, 2002.

Zim, Herbert S. et. al. *Stars*. St. Martin's Press, 2001.

Rock Hounds

www.childrensmuseum.org/geomysteries/faq3.html   The Children's Museum of Indianapolis offers this webpage listing fast FAQs about rocks and fossils.

www.mnh.si.edu/earth/main_frames.html   Provides information about "The Dynamic Earth" from the National Museum of Natural History.

http://piclib.nhm.ac.uk/piclib/www/   Natural History Museum of London.

www.sciencenetlinks.com/ebook/rocks2/rock_index.html   Offers information about different types of rocks as well as a slideshow.

Dussling, Jennifer. *Looking at Rocks*. Grosset & Dunlap, 2001.

Rhodes, Frank H. T., Paul R. Shaffer, Herbert S. Zim, and Raymond Perlman. *Fossils*. St. Martin's Press, 2001.

Shaffer, Paul R. et. al. *Rocks, Gems and Minerals: Revised and Updated*. St. Martin's Press, 2001.

Go Fly a Kite

www.cit.gu.edu.au/~anthony/kites/diamond/#intro   Provides detailed instructions for building a simple, inexpensive diamond kite.

www.idesignkites.com/   This website by kite enthusiast Michael Goddard encourages people of all ages to reach up and touch the sky through kite flying.

www.asahi-net.or.jp/~et3m-tkkw   This website provides information and pictures of Japanese kites and collections.

www.kitefestival.org   Provides information about the annual Smithsonian Kite Festival held in Washington, D.C.

www.highlinekites.com/Berkeley_Kite_Festival   This website provides information about the Berkeley Kite Festival.

www.worldkitemuseum.com   Find out more about the World Kite Museum and Hall of Fame.

www.blueskylark.org/zoo   The website where you can visit the Virtual Kite Zoo.

Blanket and a Basket

www.foodtimeline.org/foodpicnics.html   This website describes food timelines—specifically, the history of picnics.

www.picnicportal.com   Contains everything you could possibly want to know about picnics, including recipes and how to construct your own picnic table.

Deseran, Sara. *Picnics: Delicious Recipes for Outdoor Entertaining*. Chronicle Books, 2004.

Stoval, DeeDee. *Picnic: 125 Recipes with 29 Seasonal Menus.* Storey Publishing, LLC, 2001.

Walton, Rick and Jennifer Adams. *Packing Up a Picnic (Activities for Kids).* Gibbs Smith, 2006.

Chapter 3: Training Camp

Sport Camps

http://sportsrules.50g.com/ Sports Rules is a concise reference guide containing easy-to-understand explanations of the rules and guidelines of many sports.

www.sportsknowhow.com Sports Know How offers history, rules, and how-to information for a large variety of sports.

www.olympic.org/uk/index_uk.asp This official website of the Olympic Movement provides information about Olympic sports and competitions.

www.gamesandsport.org Provides rules and a history of the games we play.

Paluich, Mark (ed.). *The Book of Rules: A Visual Guide to the Laws of Every Commonly Played Sport and Game.* Duncan Peterson Publishing Ltd., 1998.

Diagram Group. *Rules of the Game: The Complete Illustrated Encyclopedia of All the Sports of the World.* , St. Martin's Griffin, 1994.

Big Splash

www.usaswimming.org Provides information about swimming at all levels.

www.ishof.org The official website for the International Swimming Hall of Fame.

www.fashion-era.com/swimwear.htm Provides information about swimsuit fashion history.

www.clubswim.com/default.asp   ClubSwim, which connects swimmers, instructors, coaches, and facilities.

www.redcross.org/services/hss/aquatics/lts.html   The American Red Cross website, which also provides a page about aquatics.

www.revolutionhealth.com/healthy-living/parenting/childs-health/safety-first-aid/water-safety   A website dedicated to keeping kids safe while in the water.

Boards and Blades

www.surfing-waves.com/beginners_guide_surfing.htm   A beginner's guide to surfing.

http://inlineskating.about.com/od/beginnerfaqs/Frequently_Asked_Questions_by_Beginners.htm   Provides information about inline skating for beginners.

http://snowboarding.about.com/cs/beginners/a/learntoride.htm   Describes how to snowboard for the first time.

http://skateboard.about.com/od/tricktips/ss/JustStartingOut.htm   Describes what you should know when starting to skateboard.

www.nsc.org/library/facts/sktebord.htm   Includes skateboarding safety tips.

www.nsc.org/library/facts/inline.htm   Includes inline skating safety tips.

www.exploratorium.edu/skateboarding   Provides information about skateboard science.

www.rollerskating.org/displaycommon.cfm?an=1&subarticlenbr=2   Provides information about the evolution of roller skating.

www.surfingforlife.com/history.html   Details the history of surfing.

www.richardschmidt.com/index.html   Richard Schmidt's School of Surfing; provides links to local surf camps.

www.surfsdsa.com   Provides information about the San Diego Surfing Academy.

www.wbsurfcamp.com/index.html   Provides information about the Wrightsville Beach Surf Camp.

www.nexgensurf.com   Provides information about NextGen surf camps and lessons in Cocoa Beach, Florida.

www2.bishopmuseum.org/ethnologydb/type.asp?type=surfboard Describes the history of surfboards.

Ride with the Wind

www.ibike.org   International Bicycle Fund; includes information about bicycle safety and bike tourism.

www.pedaling.com   Provides information including bicycle routes and trails.

www.pedalinghistory.com   Website where you can visit the Pedaling History Bicycle Museum.

www.bikeleague.org/about/index.php   The League of American Cyclists, which promotes bicycling for fun, fitness, and transportation and work through advocacy and education for a bicycle-friendly America.

www.bikewebsite.com/index.htm   Includes information about bicycle repair and maintenance.

www.cptips.com/index.htm   Provides cycling performance tips.

www.revolutionhealth.com/healthy-living/parenting/food-fitness/ active-living/kids-active/bike-safety   A webpage dedicated to bike safety.

Armijo, Vic. *The Complete Idiot's Guide to Cycling.* Alpha Books, 1999.

Meany, Terry. *The Complete Idiot's Guide to Bike Maintenance & Repair.* Alpha Books, 2001.

Off to the Races

www.usatf.org   Information provided by the U.S. Track and Field Organization.

www.runnersworld.com *Runners World* provides a personal log and running information.

www.marathonguide.com Visit this website for everything about marathons, including information, results, and a list of marathons.

www.bostonmarathon.org Boston Marathon has information and history on the marathon, qualifying times, and a list of winners.

www.rrca.org The Road Runners Club of America has a list of local running clubs.

Rodgers, Bill, and Scott Douglas. *The Complete Idiot's Guide to Running.* Alpha Books, 2003.

Game Time

www.crosswordtournament.com/ The official website for the Annual American Crossword Puzzle Tournament.

www.scrabble.com The official website of the popular board game Scrabble.

http://www2.scrabble-assoc.com/ The National Scrabble Association—a good place for learning about school Scrabble and Scrabble clubs.

www.scrabble-assoc.com/cgi-bin/wotd.pl Provides you with the Scrabble Word of the Day.

www.scrabulous.com/index.php Scrabulous—a website where you can play Scrabble online and through e-mail.

www.trivialpursuit.com The story behind the popular board game Trivial Pursuit.

www.jigsaw-puzzle.org/index.html Website for the American Jigsaw Puzzle Association.

www.chess.com Everything you've ever wanted to know about chess, including events, clubs, and online groups.

www.freechess.org A website for free Internet chess games.

www.pagat.com/alpha.html Describes the rules of various card games.

www.usplayingcard.com/gamerules/childrenscardgames.html   Provides information about children's card games.

www.hasbro.com/monopoly/   The official Monopoly website.

www.usplayingcard.com/gamerules/briefhistory.html   Gives a brief history of playing cards.

www.sudokudaily.net/history.php   Outlines the history of the popular numbers game sudoku.

www.tradgames.org.uk/index.html   Provides an online guide to traditional games.

www.customcrosswords.com/funfacts.htm   Provides fun facts about crossword puzzles.

Chapter 4: Trading Places

No Place Like Home

successfulfamilychores.com/   Provides information about how to carry out family chores successfully, including chore charts and meal planning.

housekeeping.about.com/od/involvingfamily/a/5easycharts.htm   Offers five simple chore charts.

www.happyworker.com/supermom/facts.html   Provides interesting facts about motherhood.

Reiger, Natalie. *Family: Homes, Chores, Sizes And Types.* Rainbow Horizon Publishing Inc., 2004.

Culture Shock

www.ipl.org/div/cquest   Kidspace: Cultural Quest Tour (where children can learn about different cultures).

www.kidsparties.com/TraditionsInDifferentCountries.htm   A website where children can learn about birthday traditions in different countries.

www.socialstudiesforkids.com/subjects/cultures.htm   Social Studies for
Kids; a website where children can learn about different cultures.

www.soon.org.uk/country/christmas.htm   A website where you can
learn about Christmas celebrations around the world.

library.thinkquest.org/C004179/customs.htm   A website where you can
learn about customs and traditions of clothing around the world.

Milord, Susan. *Hands Around the World: 365 Creative Ways to Encourage
Cultural Awareness and Global Respect.* Williamson Publishing Company,
1992.

Time Travel

www.socialstudiesforkids.com/subjects/worldhistorygeneral.htm
Provides a general view of world history.

www.socialstudiesforkids.com/subjects/americantimelines.htm   A
social studies website for children that provides American timelines.

library.thinkquest.org/J002611F/funfacts.htm   Visit this website for
fun facts about colonial days.

www.uspto.gov/web/offices/ac/ahrpa/opa/kids/ponder/ponder6.htm   A
website where children can learn about inventions and innovations.

cybersleuth-kids.com/sleuth/Science/Inventors/index.htm   Gives kids
information about famous inventors and their discoveries.

www.uspto.gov/go/kids/   Visit the kids' page of the United States
Patent and Trademark Office.

www.factmonster.com/ipka/A0768091.html   Learn more about children who have created amazing inventions.

http://dohistory.org/on_your_own/toolkit/oralHistory.html   A website
where kids can learn about recording oral histories.

King, David C. *Pioneer Days: Discover the Past with Fun Projects, Games,
Activities, and Recipes.* Jossey-Bass, 1997.

On the Job

www.bls.gov/k12/   Provides information about exploring careers.

www.knowitall.org/kidswork   A website where kids can explore a variety of careers and workplaces.

www.census.gov/Press-Release/www/2007/cb07ff-13.pdf   Provides interesting facts about Labor Day.

www.daughtersandsonstowork.org/wmspage.cfm?parm1=501   The official website for "Take Our Daughters and Sons to Work."

www.daughtersandsonstowork.org/wmspage.cfm?parm1=501   Offers an activity book for "Take Your Daughters and Sons to Work."

Vogt, Janet. *When I Grow Up, I Want to Be … Exploring Careers Through Music and Activities.* Heritage Music Press, 2006.

Lend a Hand

www.thevolunteerfamily.org/Default.aspx   Offers information for families about volunteer opportunities.

www.volunteermatch.org   This website offers ways in which families can find volunteer matches and make a difference in their communities.

www.dosomething.org   At "Do Something," families can learn about different causes to support and how they can contribute.

www.unicef.org/   The official website for the United Nations Children's Fund.

www.habitat.org   The official website for Habitat for Humanity.

www.redcross.org   The official website for the American Red Cross.

www.revolutionhealth.com/healthy-living/parenting/parenting-tips/family-activities/community-service   A community service website that offers a guide to families for getting involved.

Heiss, Renee. *Helping Kids Help: Organizing Successful Charitable Projects.* Zephyr Press, 2007.

Chapter 5: Creative Spirit

Paper Crafts

www.tutorials.com/06/0697/0697.asp   Describes how to learn to make paper.

www.arnoldgrummer.com   Provides information about papermaking and papermaking kits.

www.hqpapermaker.com/paper-history   Provides information about papermaking history.

Grummer, Arnold. *Arnold Grummer's Complete Guide to Easy Papermaking.* Krause, 1999.

Worrell, Nancy. *Paper Plus: Unique Projects Using Handmade Paper.* Krause Publications, 1997.

Potter's Paradise

www.hasbro.com/playdoh/   Describes creative ideas for Play-Doh projects.

www.paperclay.com   Provides tips and techniques for working with Creative Paperclay.

www.eberhardfaber.com/home_eberhardfaber_com.EBERHARDFAB ER?ActiveID=16811   Provides information about working with Fimo polymer clay.

www.sculpey.com/projects.htm   Describes various Sculpy clay projects and techniques.

www.jhpottery.com/tutorial/tutorial.html.html   Provides a beginner's guide to the art of ceramics; includes step-by-step photos.

www.factmonster.com/ce6/society/A0839922.html   Offers, interesting facts about pottery.

Kato, Donna. *The Art of Polymer Clay: Designs and Techniques for Creating Jewelry, Pottery, and Decorative Artwork.* Watson-Guptill, 2006.

Artist's Colony

www.louvre.fr/llv/commun/home_flash.jsp?bmLocale=en The official website of France's Louvre Museum.

www.moma.org/ The website for the *Museum of Modern Art* (MoMA).

www.artic.edu The website for The Art Institute of Chicago.

www3.vangoghmuseum.nl/vgm The website for the Vincent Van Gogh Museum in Amsterdam.

www.cmany.org/intro.php?pn=home The website for the Children's Museum of Art.

www.metmuseum.org The website for the Metropolitan Museum of Art.

www.artcyclopedia.com Artcyclopedia; the Internet's guide to fine art.

www.nga.gov/kids/kids.htm The website for the National Gallery of Art for kids.

Sowing Seeds

www.squarefootgardening.com Learn more about square-foot gardening.

www.thriftyfun.com/tf582744.tip.html Provides an introduction to lasagna gardening.

http://attra.ncat.org/who.html The website for the National Sustainable Agriculture Information Service.

Riotte, Louise. *Carrots Love Tomatoes*. Storey Books, 1998.

Lanza, Patricia. *Lasagna Gardening for Small Spaces: A Layering System for Big Results in Small Gardens and Containers*. Rodale Organic Gardening Book, 2002.

On Stage

www.childrenstheatre.org Provides information about the largest children's theater in North America.

www.familyfun.go.com/parties/birthday/feature/ff0707-talent-show-party/ Learn how to put on a talent show with soul.

www.musicals101.com/makemusi.htm Learn how Broadway musicals are made.

http://movies.about.com/library/glossary/blglossary.htm?terms=movie%2Bjobs Provides a movie glossary.

www.state.tn.us/education/ci/cistandards2001/music/cifatheatreartglossary.htm Provides a theater glossary.

Chapter 6: Getting to Know You

Ice Cream Social

www.sallys-place.com/food/columns/pappas/icecream_social.htm Provides recipes for an old-fashioned ice cream social.

www.ice-cream-recipes.com/index.htm Offers homemade ice cream recipes.

http://biology.clc.uc.edu/fankhauser/Cheese/Ice_Cream/ICECREAM00.HTM Provides simple directions for making home-made ice cream.

Warren, Dick, and Bobbi Dempsey. *The Complete Idiot's Guide to Homemade Ice Cream.* Alpha Books, 2006.

Dinner on the Ground

http://familyfun.go.com/recipes/family/recipe/dony78covered/ Provides information and recipes for family fun covered dishes.

www.foodandwine.com/articles/alabamas-best-covered-dish-dinner Learn more about Alabama's best covered dish dinner.

www.louisianafolklife.org/LT/Articles_Essays/creole_art_allday_singing.html Learn more about Louisiana's all-day singing and dinner on the ground.

http://familyfun.go.com/recipes/family/specialfeature/
potluck-recipes-sf/ A website offering various potluck recipes.

http://allrecipes.com/HowTo/Potluck-Show-Stoppers/detail.aspx A
website offering potluck showstopper recipes.

Siegfried, Susie. *Church Potluck Carry-ins and Casseroles: Homestyle Recipes
for Church Suppers, Family Gatherings, and Community Celebrations.*
Adams Media Corporation, 2006.

Traveling Feast

www.wikihow.com/Throw-a-Progressive-Dinner-Party Learn how to
throw a progressive dinner party.

http://entertaining.about.com/cs/dinnerparties/a/progressivedinn.htm
Provides more information about progressive dinner parties.

http://lifestyle.msn.com/FoodandEntertaining/TheWineLife/Article.
aspx?cp-documentid=686975 An article that describes "parties that
really move."

http://allrecipes.com/HowTo/Cookie-Exchange-Party/detail.aspx
Describes how to host a cookie exchange party.

Pet Parade

http://pets.aol.com/galleries or www.dailypets.co.uk Provides a gallery
of pet photos.

http://petoftheday.com/ Offers a "Pet of the Day" photo.

www.emommies.net/hats1.htm Learn more about fun hat crafts.

http://crafts.kaboose.com/wear/hats/hats-to-make-and-wear.
html Learn more about hats to make and wear.

Amateur Hour

http://fun.familyeducation.com/page/39437.html Provides more information about putting together a talent show.

www.dpi.state.nc.us/pbl/pblvidtips.htm   Learn more about tips for successful videotaping.

www.macdevcenter.com/pub/a/mac/2003/06/13/dv_tips.html.html This website provides the top 10 digital video tips.

Kent, Jackie, and Danny Kent. *Talent Shows the Kent Way: How to Put Together an Exciting, Entertaining Show Featuring Children.* iUniverse, 2003.

Block Party

www.thatsthespirit.com/en/entertaining/articles/Block_Party.asp Learn the four steps to a great summer block party.

www.ehow.com/how_135596_throw-block-party.html   Learn how to throw a block party.

www.mbd2.com/block-party-ideas.htm   Provides ideas for your block party.

Chapter 7: My Town

Walkabout

The Great City Search. Usborne Books, EDC Publishing, 2003.

Hollenbeck, Kathleen M, *Exploring Our World: Neighborhoods and Communities.* Scholastic, 1999.

Lorenz, Albert, and Joy Schleh. *Metropolis.* Harry N. Abrams, Inc. Publishers, 1996.

Macaulay, David. *City: A Story of Roman Planning and Construction.* Houghton Mifflin Company, 1974.

Sobel, David. *Mapmaking with Children: Sense of Place Education for the Elementary Years.* Heinemann, 1998.

Treays, Rebecca. *My Town.* Educational Development Corporation, 1998.

Celebrate Your Town

www.nationaltrust.org/community Learn more about the National Trust for Historic Preservation.

www.nps.gov/history/nr Learn more about the National Register of Historic Places and National Park Service.

www.nps.gov/history/nhl Find out more about the National Historic Landmarks Program.

www.nps.gov/history/places.htm Learn more about the history and cultural aspects of National Park Service places.

www.takus.com/architecture/ A website dedicated to American architecture.

Glenn, Patricia Brown. *Under Every Roof: A Kid's Style and Field Guide to the Architecture of American Houses.* John Wiley & Sons, 1993.

Founder's Day

www.nps.gov/history/nr/travel/lewisandclark Find out more about the Lewis and Clark expedition—a national registrar of historic places travel itinerary.

www.youthsource.ab.ca/teacher_resources/oral_question.html Oral history questions described by the Heritage Community Foundation.

www.infoplease.com/spot/aihmnames1.html Learn more about American Indian place names.

www.infoplease.com/spot/spanishnames.html Learn more about Spanish place names.

www.infoplease.com/spot/wackytowns.html Provides a list of wacky town names.

Back to the Future

http://pbskids.org/democracy/mygovt/index.html   Learn more about
The Democracy Project.

www.cccoe.net/govern/   Provides information about great government
for kids.

www.planning.org/kidsandcommunity/   Provides kids with community and city planning information.

http://pbskids.org/rogers/all_ages/inyourneigh.htm   The website for
Mister Roger's Neighborhood (TV show).

www.hud.gov/kids/field1.html   The Virtual Field Trip website.

A Year of Holidays to Celebrate

Some of the holidays listed here you will recognize, some are the birthdates of notable people—and some are just plain wacky (National Clean Out Your Refrigerator Day, anyone?). Choose a date and plan an extravaganza for your family. Or have fun coming up with your own wacky holiday!

January

Oatmeal Month; National Soup Month; National Pizza Week (second week); Cuckoo Dancing Week (third week)

1	New Year's Day
	Betsy Ross (1752)
	Paul Revere (1735)
3	J. R. R. Tolkien (1892)
4	National Trivia Day

5	National Bird Day
6	Joan of Arc (1412)
7	Old Rock Day
8	Elvis Presley (1935)
9	National Apricot Day
11	Milk Day
12	Work Harder Day
13	Rubber Ducky Day
16	National Nothing Day
19	Edgar Allan Poe (1809)
20	Hat Day
22	Answer Your Cat's Questions Day
23	Measure Your Feet Day
	John Hancock (1737)
	National Pie Day
25	Opposite Day
26	Australia Day
	National Clashing Clothes Day
27	Lewis Carroll (1832)
	Wolfgang Amadeus Mozart (1756)
28	National Kazoo Day
29	W. C. Fields (1880)
	National Popcorn Day
	National Puzzle Day
31	Backwards Day

February

American History Month; Black History Month; International Friendship Month; National Wild Bird Feeding Month; National Pez Week (first week); Hero Week (second week)

2   Groundhog Day

       Candlemas

3   Norman Rockwell (1894)

4   Charles Lindbergh (1902)

       Rosa Parks (1913)

6   Babe Ruth (1893)

       Monopoly board game goes on sale in stores (1935)

7   Charles Dickens (1812)

       Laura Ingalls Wilder (1867)

8   Boy Scout Day

9   Toothache Day

10   Umbrella Day

11   Thomas Edison (1847)

       Don't Cry Over Spilled Milk Day

       White T-Shirt Day

12   Abraham Lincoln (1809)

13   Get a Different Name Day

14   Valentine's Day

15   Susan B. Anthony (1820)

       National Gumdrop Day

17   Random Acts of Kindness Day

22   George Washington (1732)

25   Quiet Day

26   William "Buffalo Bill" Cody (1846)

27   Polar Bear Day

29   Leap Year Day

March

National Craft Month; Women's History Month; National Peanut Butter Week (first week); Pink Week (third week)

1   Share a Smile Day

    Peanut Butter Lover's Day

2   Dr. Seuss (Theodor Seuss Geisel) (1904)

3   Alexander Graham Bell (1847)

6   Michelangelo (1475)

9   Barbie Doll introduced (1959)

10   Harriet Tubman Day

11   Johnny Appleseed Day

12   Girl Scout Day

14   Albert Einstein (1879)

15   Ides of March

    Absolutely Incredible Kid Day

17   St. Patrick's Day

21   Spring begins

22   North American Wildlife Celebration

24   Harry Houdini (1874)

26   Make Up Your Own Holiday Day

30   Vincent Van Gogh (1853)

April

National Frog Month; National Garden Month; National Humor Month; National Be Kind to Animals Week (second week); Lefty Awareness Week (third week); National Bubble Gum Week (third week); Day of the Week Underwear Week (fourth week); National TV-Free Week (fourth week); Take Your Daughter or Son to Work Day (fourth Thursday)

1	April Fool's Day
	One Cent Day
2	International Children's Book Day
3	Find a Rainbow Day
5	National Read a Roadmap Day
6	North Pole discovered (1898)
7	No Housework Day
9	Listening Day
13	Thomas Jefferson (1743)
15	Leonardo Da Vinci (1452)
19	Humorous Day
22	National Jelly Bean Day
23	William Shakespeare (1564)
24	Pigs-in-a-Blanket Day
25	National Telephone Day
26	Hug a Friend Day
27	Tell a Story Day

May

American Bike Month; Flower Month; National Postcard Week (second week); Mother's Day (second Sunday); Bike Week (third week); National Backyard Games Week (last week before Memorial Day); Memorial Day (last Monday)

1	May Day
	Mother Goose Day
	Hawaiian Lei Day
4	Space Day
5	Cinco de Mayo
6	No Homework Day
8	No Socks Day
10	Clean Up Your Room Day
12	Limerick Day
	Nonsense Day
14	National Dance Like a Chicken Day
18	Mount St. Helens erupted (1980)
19	Circus Day
22	Sir Arthur Conan Doyle (1859)
25	National Tap Dance Day
27	Golden Gate Bridge opens (1937)
29	John F. Kennedy (1917)

June

National Adopt-a-Cat Month; National Fresh Fruit and Vegetable Month; Dream Month; National Ice Tea Month; National Clay Week (second week); Father's Day (third Sunday)

2	Radio was patented (1896)
3	First U.S. spacewalk
	Egg Day
	Cheese Day

5	First hot-air balloon flight (1783)
	National Gingerbread Day
6	National Applesauce Cake Day
9	Children's Day
10	National Yo-Yo Day
11	Jacques Cousteau (1910)
	ET movie premieres (1982)
12	Magic Day
14	U.S. Flag Day
15	Fly a Kite Day
16	National Fudge Day
17	Disneyland opens (1955)
18	International Picnic Day
19	Juneteenth
20	Ice Cream Soda Day
	Juggling Day
21	Summer begins
25	LEON Day ("Noel" spelled backward; six months until Christmas)
26	National Chocolate Pudding Day
	Toothbrush invented (1498)
27	Helen Keller (1880)
28	Paul Bunyan Day
29	Camera Day
30	Meteor Day

July

National Ice Cream Month; National Picnic Month; Parent's Day
(fourth Sunday)

1	Build a Scarecrow Day
4	American Independence Day
	Tom Sawyer Fence-Painting Day
5	Caribbean Day
6	Dalai Lama (1935)
	Macaroni Day
9	National Sugar Cookie Day
10	Teddy Bears Picnic Day
11	Swimming Pool Day
12	George Washington Carver (1861)
	Henry David Thoreau (1817)
13	Go West Day
	National French Fries Day
14	Bastille Day
15	Rembrandt Van Rijn (1606)
17	Wrong Way Day
18	John Glenn (1921)
20	First man on the moon (1969)
	Chess Day
	National Lollipop Day
21	National Junk Food Day
22	Amelia Earhart Day
24	Cousins Day

27   Take Your Plants for a Walk Day

28   Jacqueline Kennedy Onassis (1929)

      National Milk Chocolate Day

29   Beatrix Potter (1866)

      National Lasagna Day

      J. K. Rowling (1965)

August

Clown Week (first week); American Dance Week (third week); Weird Contest Week (third week)

1   Sports Day

2   National Ice Cream Sandwich Day

3   National Watermelon Day

4   National Chocolate Chip Day

5   National Waffle Day

6   Wiggle Your Toes Day

7   Sea Serpent Day

10   S'mores Day

      Lazy Day

      Middle Child Day

11   Play in the Sand Day

13   Annie Oakley (1860)

      International Left-Handers Day

15   India's Independence Day

16   Joke Day

17   Archeology Day

      Davy Crockett (1786)

18   Meriwether Lewis (1774)

       The Wizard of Oz movie premieres (1939)

22   Be an Angel Day

24   Strange Music Day

27   Mother Teresa (1910)

28   Dream Day

30   Mary Shelley (1797)

       National Toasted Marshmallow Day

September

Read a New Book Month; National Honey Month; Classical Music Month; National Roller Skating Week (fourth week); Grandparents Day (first Sunday after Labor Day)

1   Edgar Rice Burroughs (1875)

2   National Blueberry Popsicle Day

5   National Cheese Pizza Day

6   Read a Book Day

9   Teddy Bear Day

11   Make Your Bed Day

12   National Chocolate Milkshake Day

13   National Peanut Day

15   Make a Hat Day

16   Collect Rocks Day

18   National Play-Doh Day

20   Gibberish Day

21   Get Out of Town Day

22   Dear Diary Day

      Festival of the Sea Goddess

Ice Cream Cone Day

23   Autumn begins

Checkers Day

24   National Bluebird of Happiness Day

25   Salute the Sun Day

26   National Pancake Day

27   National Chocolate Milk Day

28   Ask a Stupid Question Day

30   National Mud Bowl Day

October

Vegetarian Awareness Month; Pizza Festival Month; National Popcorn Month; National Clock Month; Family History Month; World Cardmaking Day (first Saturday)

1   World Vegetarian Day

Homemade Cookies Day

2   Mahatma Gandhi (1869)

Name Your Car Day

4   World Animal Day

6   Thomas Edison shows first motion picture (1889)

9   Moldy Cheese Day

10   Double Tenth Day

11   Eleanor Roosevelt (1884)

15   National Grouch Day

16   Dictionary Day

World Food Day

22   National Nut Day

24   United Nations Day

      National Bologna Day

25   National Denim Day

28   Statue of Liberty unveiled (1886)

29   International Internet Day

31   Halloween

November

National Model Railroad Month; National Stamp Collecting Month; Peanut Butter Lover's Month; International Drum Month; Thanksgiving (fourth Thursday in November)

1   All Saint's Day

2   Daniel Boone (1734)

     National Deviled Egg Day

3   John Montague, 4th Earl of Sandwich and creator of the sandwich (1718)

4   National Candy Day

5   National Donut Day

7   Hug a Bear Day

8   Bram Stoker (1847)

9   Parade Day

11   Veteran's Day

14   National Clean Out Your Refrigerator Day

16   Button Day

17   Homemade Bread Day

     Take a Hike Day

18   Mickey Mouse (1928)

19   Lincoln delivers the *Gettysburg Address* (1863)

20   Charles Schultz (1922)

21   World Hello Day

22   Start Your Own Country Day

23   Billy the Kid (1859)

26   National Cake Day

27   Pins and Needles Day

29   Louisa May Alcott (1832)

30   Mark Twain (1835)

December

Write to a Friend Month; Read a New Book Month

1   Eat a Red Apple Day

4   Wear Brown Shoes Day

      National Cookie Day

5   Walt Disney (1901)

6   Mitten Tree Day

8   Mary Queen of Scots (1542)

10   Emily Dickinson (1830)

13   National Cocoa Day

14   South Pole Day

16   Boston Tea Party Anniversary (1773)

      National Chocolate-Covered-Anything Day

      Ludwig van Beethoven (1770)

17   First Flight at Kitty Hawk (1903)

18   Wear a Plunger on Your Head Day

20   Games Day

21	Winter begins
	National Flashlight Day
	Humbug Day
24	Kit Carson (1809)
24	Christmas Eve
25	Christmas Day
	National Pumpkin Pie Day
	Sir Isaac Newton (1642)
26	Boxing Day
	Kwanzaa begins
	National Whiners Day
28	Card Playing Day
	National Chocolate Day
	Visit the Zoo Day
31	New Year's Eve

Websites

For even more wacky holidays, check out these websites:

http://familycrafts.about.com   About.com's Family Crafts offers printable calendars with many of these dates.

www3.kumc.edu/diversity/   View a diversity calendar.

www.earthcalendar.net   View an Earth calendar.

www.rexanne.com/bday-info.html   Learn everything about birthdays.

www.famousbirthdays.com   Find a list of famous people's birthdays.

http://aol.kidsreads.com/authors/author-bdays.asp   Provides a list of authors' birthdays.

www.groundhog.org/   Offers information about Punxsutawney Phil and Groundhog Day.

My Backyard Adventures Journal

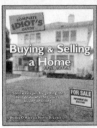

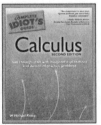